BUSINESS
IN
THE
PUBLIC EYE

by G. A. WAGNER

translated by
Theodore Plantinga

Grand Rapids
WILLIAM B. EERDMANS
PUBLISHING COMPANY

We gratefully acknowledge permission to reprint Chapter One, "Business in the Public Eye," from *Chief Executive* (Summer 1981). Copyright © Chief Executive Magazine, Inc., 645 Fifth Avenue, New York, NY 10022. All rights reserved.

Royal Dutch Shell had kindly granted permission to use their copyrighted material in some of the chapters of the original Dutch edition. The author gratefully acknowledges the assistance of his colleagues at Shell in preparing some of this material in its original form and of J. B. Beukhof for his translation of a few contributions.

Translated and edited from *Beschouwingen van een ondernemer*,
copyright © 1979 Uitgeversmaatschappij J. H. Kok B. V., Kampen

CONTENTS

PART I
AN UNDERSTANDING
OF
BUSINESS

1: BUSINESS
IN THE
PUBLIC EYE

CRITIQUE OF BUSINESS

OVER THE PAST TWO THOUSAND YEARS OF WESTERN civilization, trade and finance have often been criticized and condemned. Merchants in the city-states of ancient Greece were treated as second-class citizens. And until the end of the Middle Ages, Christian thinkers objected to interest and profit on moral grounds; important business activities were tolerated only as a regrettable necessity. Financial business in particular was regarded as sinful, an activity to be left to "others" or outsiders (e.g., Jews), whose mortal souls were of no concern to the Church. The objection was not that financiers sometimes deviated from the straight and narrow. Critics argued that financial practices were *inherently* evil.

Given the Church's enormous influence—if not complete domination of society—this view amounted to official policy. For practical reasons, of course, certain exceptions had to be made. As a consequence, the distinction between what was and was not permissible became increasingly ludicrous as economic life developed. In the end the laws of nature prevailed, and doctrine yielded to practice. Both Church and state eventually recognized business as a fundamental activity of human society—which it had been all along. The changes that this recognition prompted have had enormous social impact, in fact, the development of post-medieval Western society would have been impossible without them. Yet the debate about the moral justifiability of business—whether based on wishful thinking, ideology, ignorance, envy, or sheer malevolence—has never died away. Even today critics are asking the age-old questions. Is business good for society? Do businesses behave as they should?

Challengers focus particularly on private business, because they more readily believe that government-owned businesses, however dubious their practices, are acting in the public interest. For obvious reasons, critics most often single out larger businesses as objects of their suspicion and criticism. Thanks to the mass media, these critics find it relatively easy to get attention, to ask questions and sow seeds of suspicion, thus propagating their personal views about business. Those of us active in business must face these facts, and respond.

How are we to cope with these problems? We might feel inclined to shrug them off as annoying but essentially irrelevant, but this would be a mistake. Such problems can seriously affect the factors and responses that business depends on: political factors, the understanding of the public, the wholehearted support of employees, and the cooperation of various organizations. We might also be tempted to leave the problem to the "experts," because we executives have "better things to do", but this, too, would be unwise. Delegation does not work when a fundamental issue like this one is at stake. In short, we must meet the challenge directly.

We executives may not like it, but we cannot take for granted the continued existence of business, or a climate favorable to business. Every executive—especially the chief executive—must be able to justify his company's activities not only to himself and his colleagues, but also to outsiders. He must be able to address people of all professions and clearly explain how business perceives its value.

SOCIAL CONSIDERATIONS

Very simply, a business consists of a group of people who provide a service or a product to their customers. It uses profit as an incentive, a reward, and a yardstick to determine the efficiency, acceptability, and attractiveness of the offered product or service. The most basic social justification of enterprise is a satisfied consumer. If a business fails to "deliver," it will eventually run afoul of the law or be pressured by a dissatisified public.

Business can be described in much greater detail, but the point I wish to stress here is that business is a social phenomenon. And, like many other forms of human activity, it has a social function. Despite the egotism, short-sightedness, incompetence, and hard luck that all too often impair business operations, businesses clearly serve society by providing people with goods and services they need. Given this obvious fact, we should never accept the contention that businesspeople pursue only their own interests, while people outside the business world pursue social goals with much less selfish motives. And yet this is a thesis too frequently advanced and too infrequently rejected, even by businesspeople themselves.

GETTING THE MESSAGE ACROSS

This fact should not surprise us. The history of business is the history of people trying to make a living for themselves as owners, shareholders, and workers. Profit is essential as a reward for investment—but far too many of us have believed for too long that this was basically the whole story.

Few of our annual reports currently show how our businesses affect the public well-being. Fortunately, more and more companies are beginning to use these reports to explain and illustrate how their activities benefit society. In fact, in the Netherlands the law requires all companies over a certain size to publish an annual "social report" in addition to the customary finanical report with its balance sheet and profit-and-loss account. Actually, the entire annual report is social in its nature and its implications.

Perhaps businesspeople who write annual reports should follow this example—a suggestion that shouldn't be interpreted as sentimental or hypocritical. If we run a respectable company properly, we should not be afraid to let the significant facts speak for themselves. And when we present the social contributions of our business, which go far beyond the facts and figures required by the stock exchanges, we are also responding to the doubts and criticisms directed at us.

Explaining such contributions is important, but it is equally important to make sure that we are talking to the right people, communicating clearly and credibly. Although the annual report is essential, it has only a limited use in this regard because of its limited audience. Many of these reports have become pieces of art, containing interesting and useful information—much more than is officially required. This is fine, but we must remember who is reading these reports—almost exclusively the limited group composed of the interested, the initiated, and the professionals, including the company's employees.

The modern corporation realizes that it should address many other groups as well: trade unions, teachers and professors, journalists, the churches, the general public. And however well written and lavishly produced the annual report may be, it will not communicate satisfactorily to all these groups. Most companies are trying to reach these people through a public relations department. A ubiquitous feature of the corporate landscape, their best work is indispensable. They are run by educated professionals, people with years of business experience who can competently deal with complex problems and any type of public group.

Since many corporations have come to recognize that "public relations" is really a matter of public understanding, their public relations departments deal with public affairs in the broadest sense. What matters is not simply that the corporation maintain a good relationship with society but that it properly understand its environment— economically, socially, politically—and that it in turn be understood by as many outside groups and individuals as possible. Because this responsibility is so vast and so vital to a company's welfare, it is wisest to have the public affairs director report straight to the chief executive.

INADEQUATE PREPARATION?

I used to say, half jokingly, that businesspeople must gird up their loins "in defense of the species." By "the species" I meant private enterprise, not just one's own company. Today I fear that the stakes are even higher. The debate is now about our way of life, and in many areas we seem to be losing—a situation that increases the public responsibility resting on the shoulders of businesspeople.

Although it naturally weighs most heavily on people in senior positions, no executive can escape it.

This problem is complicated by the background of the typical businessperson. Very few executives have been recruited, trained, selected, or promoted on the basis of their ability to deal with the issues I have discussed here. On the contrary, in all but a few cases they were groomed for expertise in technology, finance, law, marketing, or one of the other areas conventionally regarded as essential to business management. I think it is wise to seek such expertise, but today and in the future it will become increasingly important to find executives who are also sensitive to human relationships, (both within and without the company), to social developments, and to political implications. Colleagues and assistants will notice those excutives who consider these factors when conducting business and shaping the company's public profile. Over time such executives should positively affect the style and image of the corporation—an influence that would benefit both business and society.

RECRUITMENT

If we agree that our executives, especially the ones at the senior level, should possess such a "social dimension," we naturally wonder where we can find such people. They are around; we can recognize them in the way they operate—in the speeches they give, in the articles they publish, in the universities where they meet the challenges of students and intellectuals, and even in the power-wielding world of television. I believe that more people than we imagine have the potential to become modern, versatile business managers, if only they are given the chance.

We must learn to adapt to this social dimension in management, and encourage other businesspeople to do the same. We should take care to practice within the organization what we preach when we are outside it, because bad relations within the corporation can damage its relationship to society. We must remember that the employees, our immediate witnesses, are, for better or for worse, the company's ambassadors.

CORPORATE PRIDE

If we are to cultivate this social dimension throughout a business organization, all who are involved must understand the complexities of both people and the world. They must also be prepared to respond to society's questions—and criticisms. I am not encouraging defensiveness, but I believe that an honest, responsible business corporation should be proud of its contribution, and should thus be willing to defend itself, which can involve frank, timely admissions of mistakes and shortcomings. Business should both listen and speak.

As I indicated, this is one of the most important concerns of the chief executive, but it is also a task for all executives, each contributing in his own way through his own area of responsibility and expertise. The effort must be a continuous one, made through all reasonable means— media included. Difficult? Yes. Impossible? Certainly not. Our biggest worry is not the doctrinaire enemy but the countless number of people who lack clear and credible information about business.

2: WHAT
IS A
GOOD BUSINESSMAN?*

THIS TOPIC IS A BROAD ONE, AND I AM WELL AWARE that many people in the business world will not agree fully with what I say. The objectivity we strive for in natural science is not always attainable in discussions of business.

DEFINITION

What do we mean when we talk about a "businessman"? I believe we should define a businessman as one who is engaged in the production or distribution of valuable goods, or who renders an economic service. As I noted in the first chapter, profit functions here as both an incentive and a yardstick. (It is interesting to note that our word *profit* is derived from the Latin word *profacere*, which, if I am not mistaken, was meant to convey "doing something for others.") If an individual is successful in providing or distributing goods or in rendering a valued service, he is a good businessman. Of course, not every good businessman is successful, because to be successful one often needs luck, which is intractable.

But what are the specific requirements for being a good businessman? He must believe in what he is doing, he

*In this chapter and throughout the book I have used this term generically, and do so simply out of ease of expression, not meaning to alienate anyone.

must possess know-how and be innovative, and he must pay attention to economic considerations. In this chapter I want to deal individually with each of these requirements.

Believing in the Job

In business, as in any other area of human endeavor, a person must believe in what he is doing. Normal people can be happy and fruitfully engaged in pursuing certain objectives only if they consider those objectives necessary or useful and reasonable, and if they think the methods of achieving them are honorable. For example, a man cannot be a good manufacturer of weapons if he considers them evil objects. Similarly, a clergyman who says that he does not believe in God can be many things, but he cannot, in my opinion, be a good clergyman. The same point applies to the methods we use in business. During wartime we tell each other that the end justifies the means; but competition in the business world is not war, though some businessmen may treat it as such. Businessmen, therefore, must believe in their methods; they must believe they are acting properly.

But how are we to determine what is—and is not— proper? This is not simply a question of personal standards; the propriety of a businessman's actions must be measured against the standards of the world in which he lives. A businessman must believe that his work is morally justifiable, and that his activities are reasonably pursued and economically profitable.

The criteria invoked in making such judgments are largely—but not entirely—on a common ground. To a certain extent it is a matter of personal belief. Some merchants will not sell alcohol on Sunday; others will not sell any*thing* on the Sabbath. It is a businessman's prerogative to make such a decision, but whatever his personal dividing line between right and wrong may be, he must also be guided by his community's standards.

This behavior does not turn a businessman into a missionary; he is simply being a responsible citizen. If he is not entirely happy with the product the business sells or with the way the business operates, he must try to make improvements. And if no satisfactory improvements can be made, then the product or service should be dropped.

Using Know-how and Innovation

A good businessman must also know his business. Normally this involves a great deal of hard work; in fact, in certain countries one even needs a diploma or two to be a shopkeeper. Of course, this may lead to ridiculous consequences, and we should certainly guard against exaggerating the requirements for engaging in business. Nevertheless, the growing complexity of modern society requires increasing know-how.

In our technological age the ever-increasing interdependence of people brings with it certain consequences— one being that an individual's actions are liable to affect the activities of many other people. Hence there must be some minimal guarantee that a businessman has some idea of what he is doing. A businessman also needs an open mind. He should always be looking for ways to improve his business, and be alert to the possibility of branching out into a related field, or starting something entirely new.

Paying Attention to Economic Considerations

In everything he does, a businessman should be especially interested in the economic aspect of business, since he is

risking his money in the hope of making a profit. Whatever the attraction of the product he is selling or the
service he is offering, it is vital that the customer be
prepared to pay a price which leaves an adequate margin
over cost; therefore, one of the businessman's greatest
concerns is the difference between proceeds and costs.
Since he can hardly influence the price, except through
the quality and quantity of the products and services he
offers, he cannot afford to relax his efforts on cost control.

Efficiency is no mere slogan; it is the *leitmotiv* of all
business, what every businessman must work to achieve.
The particular mechanics of efficiency depend greatly on
the nature and size of a company. But the common denominator for all companies striving for efficiency is the
need for hard work and an unrelenting practical interest
in proceeds and expenditures. A businessman who ignores
these matters will pay the price; he will be the first to
suffer. Yet this vulnerability is at the same time his
strength.

Economics plays a role in all aspects of business—information, planning, research, production, transportation, marketing, captial investment, operating
expenditures, staff matters, even public relations. All of
these variables must be looked at in terms of income and
expenditures. To do this properly is a tremendously complicated matter; in many cases, particularly those in which
quantification is concerned, we must exercise careful
judgment. And as we make our judgments, we must always keep in mind the economic element—whether immediate or long-term, direct or indirect, evident or
hidden—fundamental to activities of modern business.

You could rightly accuse me of being too materialistic
if I were advocating that the businessman pay attention

only to the economics of business. But, as I have already made plain, that is not my philosophy.

PROFIT

If you believe in the product or service your business is offering, and you know your field well, you will work at it if you are given adequate incentive. It is simply human nature to believe in a quid pro quo, and there is absolutely nothing wrong with this. People work for something, which for the vast majority is a monetary reward that comes along with job satisfaction (we hope) and other intangibles. Those who deny this are insincere.

For the businessman, the monetary reward is profit: thus the profit criterion is a fundamental feature of private enterprise. Profit is also the yardstick we use to judge our business decisions. Even state enterprise in communist countries is beginning to admit that nothing more accurately indicates success than profit.

The importance of economic factors is obvious when we pause to consider on what basis we make economic decisions. As I mentioned earlier, we should rely on good judgment, but to support our judgments we should try to approximate financial factors by making certain reasoned assumptions and projections. If we ignore this step, we may very probably fall prey to the kind of woolly thinking tolerated in many spheres of life, in which the optimum use of scarce resources is not the central concern. Since business operates in a competitive environment, such an approach would be disastrous.

Profit is not in itself a moral problem. We should look at the issue of profit in practical terms, because the yearning for profit is part of creation, of human nature. Profit becomes a problem, however, when an individual misdirects or abuses the quest for a return on his investment. It is the responsibility of businesspeople and the authorities to see to it that such wrong practices are avoided, and to eliminate or correct them when they develop. The perennial question, of course, is how far we should take this responsibility. Very often the answer depends on political expediency or personal interest. This matter reminds me of a story which you may have heard, but since it applies here I will tell it again.

A businessman found himself in a group of people discussing politics, economics, and social problems. Many were criticizing business, particularly the deplorable habit some businesspeople have of making continual large profits. Our friend soon realized that he was the only person there with any practical experience in business, so he decided to speak up. His declaration that he was a businessman caused a bit of a stir: people stared at him and nodded knowingly. But when he added hastily—and truthfully—that he had lost money in his business for several years running, everyone promptly relaxed, and the conversation continued pleasantly.

The businessman, then, believing in his business and striving to improve and diversify it, works hard to make a profit. But profit alone is not enough; a businessman must also be able to defend himself.

ENVIRONMENT

Obviously, businesspeople must function successfully in the world at large. They must cope with public opinion, government officials, politicians, trade unions, sociology professors, and the leaders of churches. If a businessman does not make a conscious and constant effort to know and understand his country, the world and the times, he is like a swimmer trying to ignore the water. The effort this takes is increasingly necessary—and increasingly difficult.

Today business must operate on an increasingly large scale in order to reach its commercial objectives. For this reason, if for no other, it exposes itself to public attention. Even the village butcher, baker, and candlestick-maker are much less independent of social opinion than they were a hundred years ago. When we consider the other end of the business scale (mass production), we see that the businessman's sphere of operation has become something in which politicians and labor leaders are intensely interested. This interest is spurred on by the physical network of communication, which has developed fantastically in our time (a development largely due to private enterprise itself). The result is that a corporation's actions, whether good or bad, can be made public very quickly—a factor the businessman must learn to deal with.

The businessman's dealings have become an object of study—a great deal of it theoretical, and some of it ideological. For this reason he cannot help but be interested in what happens in the universities and colleges. He is becoming increasingly aware of the need to be better understood by educators of the next generation, and also by the many other people who directly or indirectly influence his operations. No ivory tower can protect him from such influence. He belongs to a complex social whole which makes it possible for him to exist and function but which also imposes constraints. He must play the game by the rules of the environment, and with proper regard for its nature and philosophy.

What is the businessman to do—apart from minding the business? First of all, he must watch his competitors. They can be an awful bother, but it is precisely the competitor who keeps the businessman on his toes. Without competition he loses his dedication and efficiency, regardless of the sterling qualities he may possess. And any loss of efficiency hurts him and reduces the value of his service to the community. Realizing this, a businessman must support legislation against restricting competition, even if he himself suffers as a result of it. We should not try to avoid this issue by arguing that not all such legislation is wise or well applied. It is supposed to be effective, and if it is not we should criticize the formulation of the legislation, not the basic idea behind it.

Detailed information about business objectives, methods, and results should be widely distributed. Given the role that business plays in our time, secrecy in these important matters breeds suspicion, and it is dangerous if those who have the power to decisively influence business conditions are suspicious. Not long ago many businesspeople thought they could leave such matters to a handful of experts in public relations or trade relations. Nowadays we know this is not enough. Every executive in a responsible position—not just those in the public relations department—should be actively involved in explaining and defending business. And defense can even involve attack.

I would like to pass along two observations. First, a businessman's worst enemy is another businessman who behaves irresponsibly or unwisely and makes outsiders angry. Second, a businessman should think twice before getting involved—as a businessman—in politics. All too easily he can be accused of trying to pull strings to advance his own private interests. The consequences of such charges are far from pleasant—particularly in partisan politics.

When a businessman is responsible for other people's money or operates in more than one country, he should be even more reluctant to get involved in political matters. This observation may not apply fully to those who have remained fairly independent and are masters of their own ships, but their numbers are dwindling.

THE EMPLOYEE

To what extent do my remarks about the good businessman apply to the employees of a company? I can illustrate the answer by using our group (i.e., Royal Dutch/Shell) as an example. All Shell employees must believe in their company and what it offers to society. Together they must have the know-how and the innovative spirit to make the company a success. They must work hard at their jobs, at the same time showing proper regard for the environment in which they operate.

In addition to the general difficulties involved in being good businesspeople, the people at Shell have two particular challenges to face. In the first place, we have to recruit, develop, and harmoniously and efficiently employ a large number of people of many different nationalities. In the second place, we have to justify and defend our activities in a host of countries in different stages of development, countries that embrace varying philosophies of government and social order. And we must never forget that Shell, because it is a large transnational organization, is also very important to the local economy in many countries.

Though employees are not "entrepreneurs" risking capital, earning profits, and suffering losses, they are nonetheless businesspeople engaged in a business enterprise, and thus should believe in the goals and methods of the company. To foster this belief and the dedication it inspires, each employee must learn how he or she fits into the gigantic network. The learning process begins when we are recruited, and continues as we gain practical experience and our careers develop through contact with colleagues and superiors, staff channels of information, and discussion groups and courses. How much knowledge an employee acquires about the company naturally depends somewhat on his intelligence, his education, and his position, but the responsibility to know the company is imperative for everyone.

This imperative should guide our policies on information and staff development. A well-informed person is happier and better able to make a contribution to the common goal than is a poorly informed employee. Thus a good system of making information available to the staff makes excellent business sense, an incentive beyond work and pay, promotions and status.

Finally, the employee should remember the importance of his outside contacts: the impression he makes in the various situations in which he represents the company, the way he projects the company's image and defends its interests. All employees have a constructive role to play in this area, and each one should be able to make a positive contribution to the company's image.

The counterpart of this responsibility is that each employee deserves to be taken seriously: to be told things that matter, to be heard when he has something to contribute, to be promoted when he deserves it, to keep a position when he prefers it or be transferred when he wishes to move. None of this is easy to implement, but we can go a long way toward achieving our goals if we work at good human relations and effective organization.

3: POWER AND LIMITS OF BUSINESS

IN THE PROCLAMATION OF 1813 GIJSBERT KAREL VAN Hogendorp said: "All men of prominence will get into the government. . . . The common people will be given a day to make merry at public expense. . . ."

WHAT IS POWER?

In the days of this proclamation, relations between various groups—particularly the relations between various powers—were different than they are today. What is the "power" I refer to here? One of the meanings the dictionary provides is "domination over people and events." But the question then arises how strong the domination must be to qualify as power. Perhaps we should simply say that power involves exercising great influence over people and things—the ability to influence the course of events in society.

Spiritual and Temporal Power

World history has long been dominated by the issue of power. In our Western civilization we operate with the classic distinction between spiritual and temporal power. In this context the term *spiritual* has almost always meant "ecclesiastical." This was not just philosophical doctrine; it was a practical question of who was exercising authority and how that authority was to be defended. On the one side was the church hierarchy, and on the other were the

23

landowners. Each side had its assigned role and function, and each camp had its own elite, the ones who determined the course of events in society (with a power that went far beyond the "influence" I mentioned). Matters were determined by each side, together or separately.

The elitist structure (a term that should not be understood in the strict social sense) was not cleared away by the French Revolution, although it was indeed permanently changed by it. Gijsbert Karel van Hogendorp was speaking in the spirit of his time.

New Forms of Power

Over the years the above-mentioned groups became increasingly uniform. New religious views resulted in new ecclesiastical groupings, and modern political ideologies created organizations and rules that altered the the exercise of authority. This is true of liberalism and socialism, and certainly of Marxism.

In material terms, the ownership of property became a less important means of social influence. As industry rose to take the place of private, individual production, new economic groups became important. Carlyle placed his hope in the "captains of industry," who, he believed, would act more responsibly than the landowners. Then came the growth of the bureaucratic elite, the planners, and the technocrats. Today increasing attention is being paid to the issue of codetermination. Throughout this time the power of the church has steadily diminished. Although churches today indirectly affect society, their direct influence is minimal.

By stages, the liberal and socialist leaders managed to introduce universal suffrage into modern democracies. The masses then became a factor to be reckoned with; with their power they manipulated the positions of certain political leaders. Considering our general social welfare, the present parliamentary democracy here in the Netherlands is a tremendous improvement over what preceded it, despite some serious problems of implementation. Meanwhile, people continue debating how our democratic society should deal with the economic factors that determine our material well-being.

This debate is not restricted to a group of theoriticians exchanging ideas about "political economy," nor is it restricted to meetings of anarchists, agitators, and demagogues. It is a debate that is public in the broadest sense of the word.

A Conspiracy?

We hear much talk about a conspiracy; I think of James Burnham and his "managerial revolution." We are told that political leaders can no longer control the masses without relying on the money of the industrial magnates, who in turn need the political managers. "The ruling class" has become a loaded term, as has the phrase "the power elite," which C. Wright Mills has used in the title of his book. A cousin to these is the term "big brass," which Harold Lasswell uses in sketching the danger of a domineering military elite.

Certain are other thinkers oppose such talk or regard it as greatly exaggerated. In *Man and Society in an Age of Reconstruction*, Karl Mannheim argues that the elite will lose their arbitrary exercise of power; he claims that society will undergo a growing decentralization process as "organized insecurity" becomes society's focal point. Mannheim is convinced that these developments can be escaped only through a greater degree of collective planning. David Riesman does not go as far as Mannheim, but he does point to the rise of what he calls the "intellectual veto-groups," which will function as an anti-power against the elite. In *The New Industrial State*, John Kenneth Galbraith points to the establishment of a basically uniform and directionally unified "technostructure" as the end of the elite group's domination. For Galbraith this technostructure is comprised of the upper leadership in government, industry, the labor movement, and so forth. Like Mannheim, Galbraith expects that planning will replace competition.

The "Central Planners"

In Burnham's view, planning is the eventual result of the managerial revolution. Collective planning, then, really amounts to a central direction and control of the economic process. Since this is the common denominator for both the United States and the Soviet Union, Burnham expects that the fundamental oppositions between these two antagonists will eventually disappear.

Mannheim regards collective planning as the last hope for maintaining some responsible order in our mass society. He is thinking far enough ahead to be uneasy about the problem of freedom, but he has no answer to offer other than that we must change our philosophy of freedom: ". . . the new conception of freedom creates the desire to control the effects of the social surroundings as far as possible. . . ."

Galbraith wants to be pragmatic. He does not offer a theory about freedom, but when he tells us that the "technostructure" replaces competition with planning, he offers a consolation prize for the loss of freedom: through all this planning, people will have the time and means available for artistic and intellectual pursuits. For Galbraith, *homo economicus* is a grubby character that ought to be forgotten as soon as possible: "If the industrial system is only a part, and a relatively diminishing part, of life, there is much less occasion for concern." In other words, we need not be so concerned about the loss of freedom in this sphere: "We may, one time, come to see the industrial system in the fitting light as an essentially technical arrangement for providing convenient goods and services in adequate volume."

Do not think I am talking about the hobbyhorse of a handful of contemporary writers who analyze modern society. Though I have mentioned only a few of these prominent thinkers, they have countless followers in both theory and practice. Those who follow them in theory, of course, can permit themselves the luxury of keeping everything on a theoretical plane. Those who practice their theories feel called to establish laws to which others must subject themselves. If a planned economy à la Burnham, Mannheim, or Galbraith were established, we should realize that it would lead to the Soviet Union's system unless certain measures were taken and criticism was allowed.

Parliamentary Democracy
But if we recognize that man is born with a yearning for individual freedom, if we admit that he develops fully only if his individual freedom is maintained at a reasonable level, and if we bear in mind that competition is indispensable in getting people to act while at the same time keeping them within certain bounds, then we will be very careful about supporting any notion of central "planners" holding absolute and indivisible power. I am

not talking only about economic power; the objections to awarding supreme economic power to the central planners apply *a fortiori* to the larger political scene, which governs many other facets of society. Hence in the Netherlands we want a parliamentary democracy—though it still may not be our ultimate choice among all governments. In such a democracy no one is allowed to dominate on the basis of material wealth. In the final analysis, then, economic life must be subject to political authority.

If these fundamental characteristics are to be achieved in a society, it is necessary that private property be recognized, and that the means of production be wholly or largely in private hands. In this type of society (of which ours is an example), everything is relative, especially the amount of power that persons and institutions possess. Although everyone is free, businesspeople face certain limits as they work toward their goals in competition with one another: they have to honor the rules, which have been established through a democratic process.

The power people exercise in such a society is relative, because others who enjoy the same rights and obligations have set for themselves the same goal, whether it be winning the citizen's vote or the consumer's dollar. And still others have opposite goals, like those involved in the issue of dividing the national income.

POWER AND LIMITS IN BUSINESS

A government-owned business, even when it is organized like a private business, still retains its political ties. Thus the power of a government-owned business differs from that of a private business—precisely what is important in determining power and limits in business.

As I have indicated, economic powers are ultimately subordinate to political power in a parliamentary democracy. In countries that are not democratically governed, we see an even greater subordination of economic life. Naturally I do not mean to assert that in a democracy economic life is always and in all respects controlled directly by political institutions; what I mean is simply that government has the last word. The local, regional, and central governments ultimately have the final authority, either directly or through their representatives. By the latter I mean the civil service, which sometimes degenerates into a bureaucracy that seems to lead a life of its own.

A private business has to subject itself to the law and the regulations based upon that law; this in itself is proper and necessary for a balanced society. The relation between government and business is one of the most important limits of the so-called power of business, limits we see revealed at the juncture at which business encounters the public authorities.

Other limits of the power of private business also come from the nature of our democratic system. I have already mentioned competition, which is supposed to hinder the formation of economic monopolies and guarantee the consumer's freedom of choice. In addition, the labor union, which is based on the fundamental principle of freedom of association, exercises a very important power in both internal and external business relations—power that includes influence on politics and public opinion.

Public opinion, the embodiment of freedom of speech, is another factor that business must reckon with in many respects, because it affects politics, and hence the attitude of government. Moreover, public opinion and labor unions

are mutually influential. And a business lives by the grace
of shareholders, money-lenders, and clients who contribute to public opinion and the power it wields.

We will consider labor unions and public opinion later;
first I want to point out the difference between what a
business can accomplish *before* it invests its capital and
begins its operations, and the effects of these efforts *afterward*. Before making its investment, a business can demand that certain conditions be met; in other words, to
a certain extent it can shape the climate which it hopes
to develop, although competition prevents business from
overestimating these possibilities. In addition, the business is restrained by the limits set by the public authorities. (Here again, public opinion plays an important role,
just as it does at every stage along the way.) But once a
business makes a commitment by investing capital and
beginning operations, it must live with increased limitations upon which it has considerably less influence.

This description does not fit only businesses in underdeveloped countries. Nowhere in the world does an agreement on a dowry and the conditions for a marriage
guarantee the success of the marriage. During difficult
times, when "love" for business dwindles, the business's
power dwindles as well.

Just how powerful is a business, then, after it has invested its capital and made a start? At this point, to what
extent is business able to influence society? How far does
its power extend, and what are its limits?

The size of the business and its type—whether it is
national or international—does not make as much difference here as one might suppose. In the kind of society
I have been discussing, its nature and rights and obligations remain fundamentally the same. If a company grows

very large and operates in a number of countries, this generally increases its efficiency—but it also multiplies its interfaces with other powers, thereby heightening its vulnerability. In the case of a large international business, the possibilities and the opposing forces are larger and more numerous. The business becomes a player in a kind of multidimensional chess game, dealing not with lifeless pawns but with reasonable and unreasonable human beings. Fortunately, the reasonable ones outnumber the others. In short, business is necessarily involved in a community in which it must exist harmoniously with its competitors, the authorities, the workers with their labor organizations, and the public with all its diverse opinions.

Politics and Economics

The basis of private business is the political recognition of the private ownership of the means of production. This recognition is based on the conviction that competition and the decentralization of economic power are the best guarantees for the continued existence of parliamentary democracy. This does not completely rule out government ownership of business, but it clearly means that such a situation must remain the exception.

I believe that no sensible businessman will promote the notion that government-owned business is a good idea, except when it comes to public services or the so-called infrastructure. Yet we must also recognize that private business sometimes fails to such an extent that the government is forced to become involved. Such cases should certainly remain unusual; we must avoid any situation in which the political authorities directly control economic life.

In his book entitled *Morale de l'Entreprise et Destin de*

la Nation (1965; partial English translation entitled *The Enterprise Ethic*), Octave Gélinier points out that a certain interaction or reciprocal influence is essential if private business is to have any power. In politics there is a growing tendency to give social matters priority over economic matters, but limitations keep this tendency in check. This balance is important, for if we are to meet general social goals, such as providing a reasonable standard of living, social security, and full employment, and if at the same time we want our socio-economic wishes fulfilled, such as a steady and favorable climate for business, along with a stable level of growth in purchasing power—if we want all this, a constant growth in the gross national product is absolutely indispensable. Practice has generally shown that such growth occurs when a dynamic and expansive private business sector develops amid the challenges of stiff international competition. A country that has this kind of business development has the best guarantee for social progress—an assertion I make on the basis of practical experience, which I refuse to trade for theoretical negations.

Thus social as well as economic factors make it desirable for private business to flourish. (Perhaps they are the most important reasons of all.) But these social factors, which almost immediately take on political meaning, often lead to predictable consequences—that is, when private business does not flourish, the government artificially supports it and keeps it alive. This can be done in a variety of ways: one method is turning the private business into a government-owned business; a less drastic measure is the government's awarding subsidies and establishing protective tariffs, quantitative restrictions on competition.

If such measures become permanent, the country is

headed down the wrong path and will eventually suffer the economic, social, and political consequences. When the business becomes a child of the state, its vitality diminishes, and its influence (which until then had been restricted by the kinds of limits mentioned above) shifts to the hands of the state. The state thus becomes more powerful. The irony is that this situation can be prevented only if the government cooperates, because, as I indicated earlier, the basis for private business is the *political* recognition of the private ownership of the means of production.

Competition

Such cooperation means not only that the government must see to it that private business is adequately prepared to operate, but also that it must clear the way for effective competition. This means limiting the power of business, which is essential to the health of good businesses—and essential for the removal of poor businesses, those that cannot be economically justified. Of course, the social consequences of dissolving these businesses must be dealt with fairly, but this does not demand artificially extending the life of a business which can no longer survive on its own. What I am offering here is not the argument of Cain, who denied that he was his brother's keeper. The point is not *whether* we should look after others, but *how*.

I am emphasizing this point because you might say that competition is the basic article in the constitution of private enterprise. Indeed, nothing is so basic to business as competition, and the government must act in accordance with this tenet. On the other hand, competition must not create a situation in which men attack each other like wolves; it must to be reasonable. "Dumping," for example, is what I would call unreasonable competition, and the government should regulate and supervise this area of business to prevent its happening.

These ideas are recognized in many countries, and are the foundation of the treaty establishing the European Economic Community. It is not enough when the government, in the interest of national economic growth, sees to it that business is nationally and internationally competitive. Also imperative is what Gélinier calls the enterprise ethic: the entrepreneur himself must be convinced of the necessity of competition. Gélinier writes: "Cynical behavior on the part of one director of a business does more to undermine a competitive economy than a hundred Marxist propagandists." In other words, a businessman who downgrades the ethic of competition is digging his own grave.

Government

But business encounters political authority—that is, the government with its various branches—in many other areas as well. I might almost say that it bumps up against government wherever it turns. And it bears repeating that, in the final analysis, business is subject to government. In a parliamentary democracy this subjection is not absolute: certain "checks and balances" prevent the development of authoritarian totalitarianism, providing protection that business enjoys. A very pertinent question arises here: What "power" does business itself have when it comes to influencing, in its own favor, political decision-making and the conduct of government?

As I observed earlier, the answer to this question follows from the conditions that must be met in a democracy: the possession of material wealth as such must not be translatable into political power. This does not mean that a business or an association to which a business may belong cannot express political views and make government aware of them; it would be wrong to deny business a right that belongs to every other segment of a democratic society. But it does mean that a business must not use its economic resources to reach its political goals.

When a business makes a wrong move of this kind, opposing forces are called into play. Thanks to the mode of operation of a democratically organized state, these forces turn out to be stronger than the business in question. Even if the government with its administrative apparatus does not itself have the will and power to resist this sort of economic-political power—and this is sometimes the case—other opponents of the power of business—particularly labor unions and public opinion—will, directly or indirectly, come to the government's defense. The result is that sooner or later (usually sooner), the business loses the struggle.

The Labor Movement

In the modern democratic state, organized workers exercise a power which directly influences the welfare of business. They also indirectly influence business through their impact on politics and government. The real or imagined social content of the majority of the labor unions' desires is usually more attractive for politicians, publicists, and people in general than is the viewpoint of business. This pattern is always important, but it is particularly significant in times of conflict, for then business discovers (often in a painful way) just how limited its influence and power are.

Although the class struggle is an antiquated concept

in a country like the Netherlands, the philosophy of the class struggle still underlies the feelings of many people who almost invariably support "the workers." Too few of them understand why, in a modern business, the line between employers and employees cannot be so easily drawn. The reason is, quite simply, change: on the one hand, fewer and fewer businesses are run by an owner whom we could call an employer, and on the other hand, most managers in modern businesses are employees. To further complicate matters, many employees (including lower-level workers) must now be regarded as part-owners or partners because they hold shares in the company (a trend that I hope continues to grow).

Despite all these factors, most of political sympathies are traditionally on the side of the workers. People are quick to believe that businesses, driven by the profit motive, are simply egoistic pressure groups, whereas the labor unions are motivated purely by social concerns as they fight for the little man. This kind of support can result in one-sided concentrations of power that are fatal to the democratic way of life.

The fear that too much influence may be concentrated in too few hands should lead us to demand that the power of labor unions be kept in check. It would be consistent with what I said earlier to demand that labor organizations not use their economic means—the most important of which is the strike—to achieve their political goals, although it is unwise for practical reasons to make such an outright assertion. But I am willing to say this much: the political ties that some of the labor organizations have established have put organized labor in political positions so powerful that business cannot match or balance them.

Public Opinion

Public opinion is the backdrop against which all our actions and reactions are played out. Because business is well aware that favorable public opinion constitutes a tremendous advantage, it zealously seeks the public's favor, as its departments of advertising and public relations prove.

Favorable public opinion can be a valuable ally, both when specific problems loom on the horizon and when more general questions arise. And here again limits must be kept in mind: a business cannot survive very well or very long if public opinion is against it. The resulting difficulties can manifest themselves in numerous ways; critical publicity, for example, can lead to difficulties within the company, or it can give rise to external pressure. Business must reckon with both possibilities; in fact, the way a business operates is often influenced—and even determined—by such factors.

Because of the mass media, we are exposed to simple, repeated criticism of scores of people and events. Unfortunately, negative features attract more attention than positive ones, especially when the criticism is meant to "tear down." Even if companies try to defend themselves against criticism, the pall of the accusations hangs over them. Often a successful response to criticism only leaves a company vulnerable to further attack. Particularly susceptible are companies that have expanded, because size and power often go hand in hand—and power, of course, is all too easily equated with the abuses to which it sometimes leads.

We must not forget that many of the critics really do not seem worried about the continuation of our economic well-being. Besides revolutionaries, there seem to be many commentators who suppose that our social and economic achievements and potentials have somehow been guaranteed. By whom? Such commentators do not claim this honor for themselves but point to the government. Thus they are not responsible for insuring that our economic systems and institutions, for which there seem to be no good alternatives available, are kept going.

I should add that the transnational corporation is not always prepared or able to defend itself; often the defense it offers is insufficient. But even if its defense is satisfactory, outsiders have a hard time bearing the larger international picture in mind, so they still have difficulty believing that the explanation given is complete and honest. Many companies—including the rising number of transnational government-owned business—are dealing with this problem straightforwardly. They are quite willing to supply information which their critics request, but they ask for an objective evaluation—not emotional talk. And they do not want to be discriminated against simply because they are businesses.

Naturally, the tremendous growth of transnational corporations in recent years and all the good they have accomplished should not blind us to their shortcomings. On the other hand, transnational business should not be categorically condemned because of the shortcomings of certain companies. We are learning by trial and error, and we are off to a good start in international business. Blanket condemnations and rash statements inappropriate—if only because it is no longer possible to imagine our economy, which is the foundation for social progress, functioning without international business, either on the national or the international level.

The managers and directors of the transnational cor-

porations must not be short-sighted and refuse to cooperate with others in efforts to better understand and
objectively view international business. The critics of international business must avoid poorly thought-out, sub-
jective statements that create confused and negative
attitudes. And politicians must avoid adopting discriminatory measures that would advance the interests of a
sympathetic group. All of us should bear in mind that
international business is an integral part of modern society.

I wish that more of the power-holders in the media
were aware of their tremendous responsibility to help business reach the public. Perhaps we can take comfort in
the hope that such awareness will increase as they and
their organizations grow older and wiser.

SUMMING UP

If a parliamentary democracy is functioning well, a balanced society will develop, one in which various powers
oppose and limit each other. Though perfect harmony
will never exist, people of good will must all work to
gether to preserve the balance as much as possible.

I am not denying the power of business. The capital
it mobilizes, the jobs it creates, the products it develops,
manufactures, and distributes, the taxes it pays, the profits
it earns, the losses it suffers—all of this is fundamentally
important to our society. And this importance involves
influence or—if you prefer—power. Unfortunately, certain people mistakenly imagine that businesses and industries and their organizations are inordinately powerful.
People are happy to see businesses develop in their cities
and states, generating economic activity and prosperity,
but more and more they want to control and dominate

them. Often control becomes an end in itself; an example is the demand for codetermination in its extreme form.

Both business and its observers and critics must do much more to combat this tendency. My advice to businesspeople is, "Put your house in order and do not operate secretively—not with your employees, the public or the government." To know much is to forgive much. To the politician, the labor leader, the scholar, and the publicist, I would say, "Make sure you get the facts straight before you dismiss the notion that private business represents a great social good."

If the defenders of private enterprise wish to significantly help their cause, let them promote efficiency, bearing both short-term and long-term considerations in mind, and let them be open about their business. Their critics could then take comfort in realizing that the power of business has definite limits. And they might hesitate before trying to impose even more limitations on business.

PART II

BUSINESS
AT THE
TRANSNATIONAL LEVEL

4: TRANSNATIONAL BUSINESS: ITS ORGANIZATION AND OPERATION

HISTORICAL BACKGROUND

WE HAVE MENTIONED TRANSNATIONAL BUSINESS, but how would we define it? Beginning on a general level, we might say that a business is transnational if it operates in more than one country. If we momentarily restrict our focus to trade, we see that business in this sense goes back hundreds—and even thousands—of years, and included sea travel and transport of goods. The ancient Phoenicians were active in international business, and so were the merchants of the Hanseatic League in the Middle Ages.

The international financial system began its gradual evolution in the late Middle Ages. During the nineteenth century, it made a substantial contribution to such developments as the growth of the United States. An interesting example of an international banking firm successful at this time is the House of Rothschild. (I am assuming that this family, which consisted of various independent "units" in different places, can be regarded as a single business enterprise.)

Although trade, sea travel and transport, and finance have been carried on for centuries on an international basis, the same cannot be said of production. Without

43

declaring King Solomon's mines to be either fact or fiction, we can say that businessmen first began large-scale production *outside* their homeland during the period that later came to be called "colonial." In recent history, trade with non-Western countries has led almost automatically to foreign companies' establishing manufacturing plants in those countries. Over a period of time, this development inevitably took on certain political connotations. The result, in the twentieth century, is criticism—some of it justified, and some of it not.

Gradually these colonial patterns in economic relationships have disappeared. (I will not be considering the relationship between the economies of certain communist countries.) This process of economic change was already underway before the political bonds were broken or completely modernized.

During the past eighty years, more and more companies have been expanding their activities beyond their homeland. This kind of expansion was particularly prominent after the second world war, when, during postwar reconstruction, countries helped each other with money, raw materials, machinery, and labor. All of this stimulated the growth of international business.

Other growth factors were also at work. Technical developments created new possibilities for the use of raw materials by modern industries. As the system of transportation grew, more and more bridges were established between various countries, with the result that the different phases of the production process could be carried on in various locations. Mass consumption called for mass production, and vice versa.

We could say that the world grew smaller and smaller, or that the economic network—including production, transportation, and consumption—grew ever larger. I speak here of the *economic* network, because the *political* boundaries did not expand—not even in Europe, which was so eager to lead the way in creating newer and larger political units. On the contrary, in many parts of the world the existing political units were divided, and the domestic economies involved almost invariably suffered.

Nevertheless, it can surely be said that economic activities are increasing beyond national and continental boundaries. The modern business enterprise has shown human qualities: it wants to develop and grow and become strong. And once a company's capacities develop to a certain point, the company can only progress by increasing its scale of production, transportation of goods, and trade.

THE MODERN TRANSNATIONAL BUSINESS

International economic and commercial relationships have developed considerably over the years. The simple trader exporting to foreign markets has evolved into a company with subsidiary companies and manufacturing facilities outside the country of origin. This trend was already apparent before the second world war, but the multiplication and growth of transnational corporations became especially vital after 1945, when the coming of peace opened borders and permitted the involvement of additional countries.

Investment abroad has contributed greatly to the development process in both industrialized and developing countries. Transnational business was successful because it provided a "package"—a combination of human skills (particularly in technology and management), money, and a willingness to venture into new fields, despite the added risk and uncertainty encountered by companies operating in foreign countries.

Such developments have been possible only with the agreement—and the encouragement—of governments. The impetus for investment abroad has come in part from companies seeking to employ their resources efficiently and profitably, and in part from governments, especially those of developing countries. Such governments have competed with one another through tax incentives to attract the scarce resources of investment. Certain bilateral agreements have facilitated the establishment of companies in countries that are party to the agreement on a reciprocal basis. In Europe, for example, the Treaty of Rome has encouraged the spreading of industrial investment throughout the member countries.

A large part of the economic and commercial activity that now crosses frontiers is conducted by groupings of companies. Each member of such a group carries out its business in the country in which it is located and is subject to the laws, regulations, and customs prevailing in that country. Foreign investment of this sort has succeeded particularly well in developing countries, because it has developed resources and provided services which would otherwise have remained undeveloped and unavailable for some time.

These subsidiaries in developing countries hold no privileged position; the economic opportunities they seize are also open to any nationally-owned companies. In industrialized countries, foreign-owned companies also compete with local companies. If they are successful in competition, it is because they have more efficient management or better research capacities, in which case their success contributes to a general raising of efficiency.

Such groups of companies have grown as a result of various individual investment decisions. Each such decision requires the implicit or explicit consent of the government of the country in which the investment is to be made. In the case of the European Economic Community, the individual countries consent to investment by agreeing that the right of establishment is one of the fundamentals of economic cooperation.

The companies commonly called "transnational corporations," vary immensely. Since their variety is far more striking than their similarities, general definitions tend to be misleading. A definition that should be acceptable, though, is that "transnational enterprise" involves foreign investment, the relationships between parent companies and subsidiaries, and the conduct of related economic activities. In other words, "transnational enterprise" seems to be foreign investment on a large scale.

The transnational groupings of companies do have a special contribution to make: each local unit or company benefits from the experience of other companies in the group, which have operated in a variety of circumstances. Advances in the technology for discovering and subsequently developing oil, for example, have been greatly stimulated—to the benefit of the countries concerned—by experience which could not be gained on a purely national scale.

Most economists believe that transnational business is here to stay. Its contribution to world development is significant, although it is not without problems. But it is important to isolate the substance of these problems from emotional reactions to them; otherwise it is possible that

the valid contribution that such business makes will be
frustrated by actions based on ignorance or misunderstanding. Transnational corporations themselves must play
a significant role in eliminating these misunderstandings.
They must conduct themselves properly and openly provide information about their activities. In the final analysis, the only sure basis for survival is mutual advantage:
companies have no power beyond this to ensure their
own survival.

Economies of Scale

It is not hard to see why Americans made such an early
start in the frequent and consistent use of economies of
scale: their gigantic market and their wealth of raw materials pointed in that direction. And whether we are
talking about local, national, or international companies,
the pressure to move toward economies of scale still exists
today.

As we look around, we can easily see how difficult it
is for small and intermediate-sized companies to stay in
business. Every year, countless small businesses collapse—
the efforts of butchers and bakers, small-town tradesmen,
and many others. It may well be that we must regard this
as a social and cultural loss, but it is very hard to do
anything about it. The victims are mourned only by their
neighbors and by those who were involved in the business.

We should also note that the newspapers are full of
announcements about mergers—worth reporting because
they may involve venerable names and a large number of
employees, or because people have conflicting opinions
about them. Companies merge (*merger* is often a euphe-
mism for *absorption*) in order to become bigger, stronger,
and more efficient. Of course, if a merger involves com-

panies of separate national origin, it has the same basic economic justification, but another aspect always enters the picture—the relationship between local interests and an unknown force or organization from "outside." In short, politics plays a role.

This is not a new phenomenon, but the political dimension is becoming increasingly prominent today. Because international business is moving into new areas and becoming active in countries where it was previously unknown, it is attracting more attention than ever before. It is receiving both appreciation and criticism, support and opposition—which is to be expected when business is active in so many areas at once.

Of course, even the growth of international business has its limits. It has been predicted that by the end of this century, industry and commerce will be dominated by 200 to 300 gigantic companies. This would mean an age of economic mastadons, a time in which small businesses could not survive. But I do not believe that such predictions will come true, because too many external forces are working against any such development. After all, there is a limit to the activity a single company can control: it is not easy to simultaneously exercise effective control over concurrent activities in many parts of the world. I also believe that the economy of the future will leave an important place for small and intermediate-sized companies, though they may be somewhat larger than their predecessors.

One of the factors that must be reckoned with is the legislation forbidding monopolies. Such legislation is not aimed specifically at large companies or transnational corporations, but it certainly does not exempt them, either. Transnational corporations have to obey those laws.

For more details on this issue, I refer you to a report undertaken and published by the International Chamber of Commerce—a study in which I was privileged to participate. The report is based upon the congress meeting in 1969 in Istanbul, which had as its theme "International Economic Growth: The Role, Rights and Responsibilities of International Companies."

Formal Organization

The majority of all large international corporations distinguish between organization in the formal, legal sense (corporate structure) and organization in the material sense. I want focus on the formal organization first.

In a corporate structure, the feature we first think of is the so-called holding company, which owns shares in operating companies. In the simplest model, we have a single holding company in one country with operating companies in various other countries. In actual practice the situation is often much more complicated: the holding company may be a sister of other holding companies, and its "daughters" may in turn hold shares in other companies. We face still more complications when partner's are involved, either in the holding company or the operating companies or both.

In most cases, such businesses follow this rule: employ the most efficient legal structure possible in the country in which the "holdings" are located, or where the actual operations take place. In most cases the best structure is the limited liability company. The fiscal situation, which varies from country to country, plays a role in the choice to be made. Naturally, one would want to use the structure that keeps the tax burden as low as possible. Another factor is the delimitation of the various rights and interests of the partners. Moreover, it is sometimes necessary to give part of the business its own identity; for this purpose it might be wise to set up a separate company.

Still other factors are involved. For example, some corporate arrangements are a result of situations that no longer exist. In such cases the managers of the business would be wise to consider "corporate simplification," a kind of "purification" that can often lead to healthy results. A by-product of such simplification is that the structure of the business becomes easier for society to understand, and thus may prevent misconceptions from developing.

The need for openness should be underscored, because the large business enterprise is an important part of society. In many cases a complicated corporate structure cannot be avoided, but we often see that the company's family name is maintained in the names of the related companies so that not only the authorities (governments have a way of finding these things out) but also the general public know with whom they are dealing.

The national "components" of an international business must obey the laws and other demands that are in effect in the places where they operate. If a business is not strictly loyal to the law of the land, it loses the right to exist. Scrupulous attention must be paid to local regulations, and businesspeople should take pains to avoid creating the impression that their foreign operations border on the impermissible.

One of the implications of such a code is that the principle of legitimacy must be strictly observed during times when governmental authority is being challenged. Deviation from this rule is justified only by *force majeure*, by some series of events that could not be anticipated and

cannot be controlled. Whenever an international businessman forgets this principle and allows his own political
sympathies and antipathies to influence his decisions, he
is acting out of turn. He is then violating a taboo of the
business culture: forgetting that he and his company are
guests in a foreign land.

But what, exactly, constitutes *force majeure*? This is
not a simple matter, especially not in the context of international business. But one piece of excellent advice
was given to me when I was handling a delicate matter
in foreign business: "You may consider your company in
a situation of *force majeure* when you can see the white
of the other fellow's eyes." Matters would certainly be
simpler if corporate law didn't vary so much from country
to country. Some valuable studies of this issue are currently being done, especially within the framework of the
European Economic Community. Yet international business has learned to live without an international code of
corporate law, and on the whole it has worked out quite
well.

Much more important would be establishing international fiscal harmony. In this area relatively little has
been achieved apart from some very valuable bilateral
treaties designed to eliminate double taxation. The intro-
duction of a value-added tax in the European Economic
Community was a step in the right direction, but much
remains to be done—legislation is lagging behind
experience.

Submission to local legislation must also be a guarantee
against the use of unreasonable economic force, which is
feared by many. When regional economic regulations are
in effect, as they are in the European Economic Community, all the parts of an international company located

within the region must abide by them. The mother companies are practically and legally bound to play the game according to the rules; moreover, on legal and ethical grounds they are obliged to see to it that their daughter companies stay in line—today, tomorrow, and as long as they exist. It is clearly in their own interest to do so.

Fortunately, it is not often that the government of the country in which a certain company is located pressures that company in an effort to influence certain activities carried on by related companies in other countries. As I see it, this sort of thing is legally debatable, politically unwise, and can cause embarrassment to the company concerned. It ought to be stoutly resisted.

Material Organization

As I have indicated, the material organization of a company is another matter. What we are talking about here is the division of labor among the various "units" of the company. Within the boundaries of what the legal structure allows, efficiency is both the goal and the rule.

The operating company that manufactures products in a certain area or engages in various other industrial or commercial activities there is required to give an account to its shareholders through the holding company. The operating company makes plans, invests, produces, builds, buys, and sells in consultation with—and often with the help of—the holding company. This "help" may be given through clearly defined tasks of special daughter companies, often called "service companies." And the *advisory* task of the central office can be very broad. It can provide expertise in such areas as production, construction, commerce, planning, computer application, and management.

The central office of an international company may,

on its own, undertake activities that are not left to the so-called local operating companies. Take, for example, sea transport. This is an area of activity which an international company would not want to see divided up among the various local companies unless the law in certain countries required it. In other words, if such business can be conducted on an international basis, then it surely will be. Another example is "research," which—for obvious reasons—ought to be carried on as much as possible at a central location. People in various parts of the world can be consulted, but the actual work of research should not be spread over many separate locations. Also in this category is the central control of finances, those financial operations not left in the hands of the daughter companies. A final example is the central recruiting and training of the international staff.

Finally, a holding company can decide to promote efficiency by channeling its relations with operating companies through one or more regional organizations which are then the focus for all contacts with daughter companies operating within the region. In this manner the center obtains a coherent overview of its operations, and quick action becomes possible through continuous consultation at an international level, both vertical and horizontal.

I must add a few words about responsibility and authority. The holding company, as shareholder, naturally has some rights in relation to the operating companies, which are in turn accountable to it. But the operating company is autonomous within its own jurisdiction. In its internal relations with sister companies and advisors, the mother company, and the "grandmother" company (if there is one), its autonomy must be respected. This is, among other things, a matter of economic necessity.

When a conflict arises between the international company and a national daughter company (or when it appears that a conflict will develop), those in charge must be prepared to properly inform all the people involved in the dispute, whether they are within the company or outside it. Executives must also be willing to listen to these people. I know from my own experience how many problems can be prevented or solved if such a policy is followed.

The Elements of an International Business

International business has the same elements as any other business—namely, the entrepreneur, capital, and labor. All three are necessary, so I have made no effort to put them in a logical order. The chicken-and-egg question is child's play in comparison with the much disputed question of the relative importance of each element.

When we talk about a large international business, we can no longer distinguish the *entrepreneur* from capital and labor. Naturally, much depends on how we define a "large" business, but in the case of the very large international companies, surely, we no longer find a single individual or a small group exercising control on the basis of ownership. For the largest businesses, then, the so-called managerial revolution is complete. In the financial sense, the entrepreneur is actually all of the shareholders, who are risking their money—and very large businesses have numerous shareholders.

When it comes to the controller of the business, the "entrepreneur" is usually a group of people, no one of whom exercises absolute authority—not even internally.

The people making up this group have usually come from the company's labor force; the manager of a large international business, for example, is often an employee who has reached the top through numerous promotions. The largest companies have become too big for owner-entrepreneurs.

The *capital* with which the business is started usually comes from one country, where it is initially invested and put to work. Later some of the capital is also put to work in other countries. As the business grows, and it becomes increasingly difficult to maintain finances at the right level, the controllers seek a broader base.

It is desirable for a business to finance itself as much as possible and to provide its own capital for expansion. Such self-financing is one of the reasons why—specifically in the case of a growing company—only a certain percentage of the net profit is turned over to the shareholders. This rule applies especially to a large international company.

A truly international company tries to find shareholders in many countries, something it does by offering shares for sale on stock exchanges where the issues of stock can appeal to all sorts of investors. Unfortunately, in many countries it is difficult to get the public interested in investing money in an international business. One must contend with a conservatism that can only gradually be overcome. Many companies have responded to this problem by reducing the nominal value of their shares so that small investors will be able to buy them. This move has made it easier for these companies to put together the needed capital, and at the same time has promoted an interest in the industry and the companies among a much broader segment of the population. Such action stimulates the growth of democratic capitalism. In addition, when a company undertakes a joint venture with investors in another country, whether large or small, it generally makes influential people in that country more knowledgeable about and sympathetic toward business.

Of course, a business can borrow money, but it should follow certain limits when doing so. Some businesspeople regard long-term loans for up to twenty-five percent of the needed capital as rather high proportionately, but others are willing to go higher still. The general guideline is that a healthy balance must be maintained between a company's own money and borrowed money.

Because of the enormous amount of investment activity, especially in the last ten or fifteen years, more and more companies are drawing on the capital market. In the process one observes that the internationalizing of the companies involved brings with it the internationalizing of their financing. As we all know, many people regard the rewarding of capital as problematic or somehow dangerous. Though we may regard this as a short-sighted, narrow-minded view, it does exist, and is zealously propagated—especially by people who do not understand business very well. Complicating this problem is the international aspect of business: the matter of investing (and all that investing involves) in a "foreign" country. Often the foreign country is a developing or underdeveloped nation—one that is having a hard time keeping its head above water. And many people think it is wrong that foreign investors make significant profits on the capital they have invested in such places.

When we ponder such situations, we should remember that if an entrepreneur has some capital available, he does not have a hard time finding a place to invest it. His money is welcome almost anywhere he turns. Usually he can find favorable conditions for investment, especially in a country where there is not yet much economic activity. The problems usually arise when the capital and the labor involved turn a profit, and when the time arrives for the transfer of depreciation and dividends. This time does not always come early in the history of a company, because in many cases the depreciation and profits are held within the business for a while; and when the time for a certain amount of transfer comes, obstacles may have developed. What can be done about this?

The key is good planning. The entrepreneur must think carefully about what he is doing *before* he begins to operate in a foreign country. And from the very beginning he must see to it that the officials with whom he must deal in order to do business know exactly who he is, what he is doing, and why he is doing it. They must have insight into the important aspects of his business, because a business that is largely unknown will not be much appreciated; it is simply a mistake to operate secretively.

The businessman's strongest argument is that his business serves the interests of the country in which he is operating, but he must be able to demonstrate this assertion. He can perhaps point to increased production in his field, an increase in which his company played a role. Perhaps he can also point to jobs that have been created, the training received by local employees, and the earning of foreign currencies through exports. In addition, he can emphasize the multiple benefits of these factors: the stimulation of other economic activities, the social development, the growth of knowledge, and so forth.

In short, the businessman must be able to show that his company is contributing to the development of the country. If he follows such a policy, as I indicated earlier, it will carry him a long way. Trust must always be the basis for healthy social relationships, especially commerce and industry. True, the businessman can also rely on investment treaties, credit insurance, and international arbitration agreements, such as those worked out under the auspices of the World Bank. These are all praiseworthy mechanisms—but one sincerely hopes that their provisions will not have to be implemented.

The third element of international business is *labor*— the employees or workers. In the case of most businesses that have gone outside their original borders, the original employees are drawn exclusively from the homeland. Over the years, as a sensible international company expands, it strives to attract as many local employees as possible in each country in which it operates. Not only do the various countries' governments appreciate such a policy, but it also benefits the company, because these employees can be counted on to know the local circumstances best.

An international company should not reserve the most important positions for employees who represent the land of its origin; it should simply strive to find the best qualified people for the positions available—citizenship aside. Naturally, this rule has exceptions, cases in which another approach is needed because of local legal or political circumstances.

It is also possible to make a mistake in the opposite direction: to insist that in each country an international business must put its branch or operating company under the management of people who are citizens of that country. In certain nations such a policy would be unwise simply because people have more confidence in foreigners. Admittedly, such situations are exceptional, but they do exist.

I have already indicated that a company belonging to an international group must subject itself fully to the local laws and other rules. Naturally, this includes social legislation. In recent years a movement has developed—and is especially strong in Europe—in support of worker participation or codetermination (*Mitbestimmung*, as the Germans call it). In some countries this idea—giving employees a share of company authority—has been implemented in numerous ways.

In the case of an international business, however, this issue may have an extra dimension, because the company may be active in various countries—some of which may have vastly different attitudes toward codetermination. I believe that great caution is called for here. If a mother company decides to support codetermination, it must consider the possible consequences for its divisions or daughter companies operating outside the homeland.

5: TRANSNATIONAL BUSINESS AND INTERNATIONAL RELATIONS

CHARACTERISTICS OF THE OIL INDUSTRY

SOME BUSINESSES HAVE VIRTUALLY ALWAYS BEEN active in more than one country because that was the only way they could operate. The oil industry is one such example. Some of the greatest deposits of raw materials were found in areas where there was no market to speak of, and in countries with a demand for oil there were no raw materials. As a result, the main areas of production are not in the same part of the world as the main areas of consumption. This calls for a complex exercise of matching supplies to the needs of the market place. For reasons of competition and economics, this has usually led to the growth of companies integrated all the way from the wellhead to the consumer. I believe this has proven to be the most efficient way of meeting the demand for oil.

The Royal Dutch/Shell group of companies is one of the largest of such groupings, with investments located in many parts of the world. I think it is important to examine the reasons which, over the years, have led to its present shape.*

Oil companies first have to search for oil in areas where geological indications signal its possible presence. The

*See p. 121 for the Statement of General Business Policies.

location of refineries, distribution facilities, and marketing outlets is determined basically by economic development, since there is a close relationship between the degree of a country's economic development and the amount of energy it consumes. Logistics also plays a decisive role in these matters. It is external factors of this kind that largely determine the location of an oil company's investments.

The Royal Dutch/Shell group of companies comprises a very large business, but I do not believe that in this instance size can be equated with power, as popular myth would have it. The group's investments, varying in size from country to country, are considerable; but they cannot simply be added up as an aggregate of power and compared with a country's gross national product or total income. In addition, once an investment is made in a certain area—in production, refining, or pipelines, for example—it usually remains there for a very long time. The company making the investment must therefore develop policies and practices that will make it a good "citizen" who is accepted and respected over the years. Thus, if anything, investments of this magnitude are hostages to fortune.

Because different host companies establish different conditions, a group of companies like Royal Dutch/Shell makes a variety of working arrangements. These may include wholly-owned subsidiaries, majority-owned affiliates with local public shareholdings, and partnerships with government as the major partner. These relationships evolve with the passage of time. The problem in observing them is that just as newspapers fail to comment on the thousand aircraft that safely cross the skies but single out the one that crashes, critics of business tend to virtually exclude the innumerable examples of successful and enduring relationships in business, and concentrate on the tensions that sometimes develop in international business arrangements.

When a dispute occurs, for whatever reason, it must be apparent to all that the sovereign power of government is paramount. There is ample evidence of government's power and of the impotence of a company or its parent in some other country—often in small sovereign states offering little compensation that must be judged inadequate by the standards of international law. Shell companies have been expropriated in Algeria, Ceylon, Cuba, Egypt, Guinea, Libya, Somalia, Syria, and South Yemen; only in a few cases was there adequate compensation.

Faced with the reality of sovereign power, it is vitally important for an international company to behave acceptably. I believe this can best be achieved by delegating authority to the management of each company, thus making it possible for the actions and decisions of the local managers to meet the requirements of their particular environment.

Decentralization

Part of the reason for the success of Shell managements in achieving compatibility is the long-standing policy of substituting local nationals for "imported" personnel at all levels. In the top executive group of company managements around the world, nationals outnumber nonnationals by two to one. This process started in the Shell group of companies long before governments began introducing stringent regulations for work permits. I regard this policy on Shell's part as simply a logical development in Shell's adaptation to local environments.

In the area of social and industrial relations, the successful local management must have an aware, responsible attitude toward local needs and requirements. Thus the Shell companies have developed a wide range of training programs which are by no means confined to providing skills in oil technology. For example, individual companies train electricians, fitters, machinists, welders, motor mechanics, ships' deck and engineering officers, computer programmers, accountants, geologists, and mechanical and civil engineers. If appropriate professional training facilities are not available locally, the companies provide opportunities to study abroad. In fact, many students from developing countries are sent to industrialized countries to study under Shell sponsorship. And sometimes the companies make financial contributions toward the establishment of local academic institutions.

Conditions of employment must be shaped mainly by the environment in which a company operates. Industrial relations, policies, and bargaining can only be carried out within an existing national framework; they cannot be dictated from some faraway headquarters.

It is the clear policy and practice of the Shell companies to recognize trade unions that represent the majority of employees in a common interest group. In fact, I think the growth of trade unions throughout the world has been helped—not hindered—by the growth in international investment spearheaded by companies like Shell.

Planning and Decision-Making

In our business, planning starts with the market; it starts with anticipated consumer demands which we must meet—not create. Success in meeting the demand for oil requires a fully competent authority for the local operating company.

One of the fears sometimes expressed about transnational corporations is that they make decisions concerning significant parts of a country's economy from some remote headquarters. But the fact of the matter is that running a large organization in such a manner would be inefficient and would court local nonacceptance. True, the local management must discuss expenditure of capital above certain discretionary levels with the shareholding company when the latter's finances, guarantee, or credit are involved. Nevertheless, it must be remembered that investment decisions are made in response to opportunities that are almost invariably generated by the local management (except in those instances in which the investment is being made for the first time). Such opportunities might arise, for example, from the demand for certain products, or from the suspected existence of resources and a company's perception of what it believes to be a chance to put its skills to work. The direction of investment is dictated by the opportunities in a given nation—opportunities that are open to all who have the capacity to make something of them.

Although each local company reflects the needs of the area in which it operates, there are of course some areas in which uniform practice strengthens all companies of a group. Safety precautions, for example, should be consistently followed. And conservation and environmental protection are vitally important in any area; pollution is no respecter of national boundaries. In short, international problems require international solutions.

Oil companies have already made substantial contributions in this field. Preventing oil pollution in the oceans is a major concern, because a great deal of work must still be done to undermine this constant threat.

MISCONCEPTIONS

I will now discuss three problems that develop because of the false belief that transnational corporations operate beyond the law and can evade the jurisdiction of any sovereign state. First, it is alleged that they have the flexibility to make and move investments at will. Second, they are said to be able to switch profit-centers from high tax areas to low tax areas. Third, we are told that they are able to increase their profits by taking advantage of certain opportunities to manipulate transfer prices.

If a company's physical assets are small, it may be possible for the private foreign investor to remove them under certain circumstances. But it is clearly impossible to move a refinery or a production operation at will. Once the investor has undertaken such a venture, he is the prisoner of his investment. The only real power the investor has is the power *not* to invest. In a competitive industry, of course, someone else may then take up the opportunity he has turned down.

Some people fear that affiliates can make transactions which can move profits from high tax areas to low tax areas, thereby evading the fiscal regulations of the host countries. This is a genuine source of anxiety. But such fears could be allayed if governments would work to achieve greater uniformity in tax law and practice and would extend the network of double-taxation agreements with their anti-avoidance provisions. It should be remembered, however, that one of the disadvantages of foreign investments is that the investor runs the risk of being taxed twice on the same profits—an occurrence that is not unusual. Avoiding such double taxation is a legitimate objective.

As for the question of transfer prices, any manipulation in the oil business would almost certainly be detected and challenged because of the growing awareness of transfer prices and the availability of a third-party market, which can serve as a yardstick for pricing in transactions between affiliates. Moreover, government authorities have powers in this area, and since oil imports constitute a significant charge on foreign exchange earnings, they have quite an incentive to exercise those powers. Thus, if governments wish, they can be fully aware of the transactions made by local affiliates of transnational corporations, and can satisfy themselves that the transactions are commercially based and conducted at "arm's length." It is desirable, of course, that companies should have their transactions based on arm's-length commercial agreements which can be fully justified to governments; this is the policy of the Shell companies.

It is also worth noting that if companies could indeed practice the flexibility of which they are accused, their overall effective tax rate would be lower than it is. As things actually stand, the refusal by one fiscal authority to accept transfer prices at a level required by the authority handling with the other side of the transaction often leads to an artificially high effective tax rate.

The primary safeguard against the possibility of manipulation is the right of the respective fiscal authorities to disallow a price. It has been suggested that tax officials in developing countries do not have sufficient expertise in such matters. If this is the case, it may be that special training should be introduced, perhaps with the assistance of U.N. agencies. In addition to protecting national interests, this more informed approach would help eliminate those irregular situations that occur when fiscal authorities differ on the acceptable pricing levels.

A further charge is that companies in transnational groups can increase the pressure on a weakening currency or an increasingly strong currency by moving their liquid resources to their greatest advantage during a period of strain. Though this charge is difficult to support either way, it appears to be greatly exaggerated. An efficient company will maintain its working capital at the minimal level consistent with the requirements of the business. In a competitive industry such as oil, the retention of unnecessary liquid cash resources for the purpose of speculating on foreign exchange would quickly make any company uncompetitive. Thus it is unlikely that individual companies or companies in groups indulge in such activity.

Of course, it must be recognized that a good manager will do his best to husband the value of his company's financial resources. The aggregate impact of such husbanding by all companies—whether foreign or nationally owned—that have or need foreign currency might conceivably have some impact on swings in the value of foreign currencies. But the point has not been proven either way, and, in any case, any such impact is likely to be much less significant than the impact of the operation of banks and other institutions that deal in money.

HOME AND HOST COUNTRY PROGRAMS

The definite problem plaguing home and host countries is the matter of extraterritorial application of domestic legislation. Certain countries treat the foreign subsidiaries of the companies incorporated in their territory as extensions of the parent firms and then use their policies to affect the behavior of the affiliates. If such practices are to continue, it should be with a full understanding of the effects on foreign affiliates and ultimately on the host country.

Although it might seem desirable to discourage the extraterritorial application of domestic legislation, I do not believe governments would be ready, on either legal or political grounds, to give up their right to intervene diplomatically in order to protect their citizens and their property rights. For some countries, surrendering such rights would involve considerable—if not insuperable—political and constitutional difficulties. Considering these factors, it seems unrealistic to invite individual governments to legislate their acceptance of the principle of the Calvo Doctrine. This doctrine is without support in general international law and has found no recognition outside a certain geographical area.

The World Bank, in its *Convention on the Settlement of Investment Disputes Between States and Nationals of Other States*, points to a solution which, while giving limited recognition to the Calvo principles, at the same time provides machinery which could be used to give foreign investors greater confidence and security. Article 27 of the *Convention* declares that contracting states are not to give diplomatic protection or make international claims concerning any dispute which one of its nationals or some other contracting state has submitted or consented to submit for arbitration under the *Convention*. Moreover, the right to diplomatic protection in these circumstances is limited to informal diplomatic exchanges for the sole purpose of facilitating a settlement of the dispute.

The U.N. Secretariat's report, entitled *Foreign Investment in Developing Countries* (1968), contains a significant recommendation in favor of bilateral investment protection agreements. We read that "the spreading acceptance of bilateral investment treaties, adapted to the particular conditions and relations of each pair of countries and often coordinated with concrete investment projects, may point to a more realistic method for providing international law protection to investors." This recommendation seems to have been widely accepted, because there are now a great many treaties or agreements of this kind between developed and developing countries. A few of these agreements have even been made between two developing countries. To the extent that the developing countries are increasing their external investments, an increase in the number of agreements between them can also be anticipated.

DIALOGUE AND EXCHANGES OF INFORMATION

Is a permanent international forum necessary to deal with matters of this sort? The wisdom of establishing still more institutions can, of course, be questioned. Yet I welcome the idea in principle, because it would allow the dialogue—and I do mean *dialogue*—concerning transnational corporations to take place on a continuing basis.

I have one reservation: such dialogue should not be exclusive. By this I mean that national enterprises over a certain size should also be included in the dialogue. Just how transnational corporations differ from national enterprises in their operations is not always easy to determine. Exactly what is the distinction between these two types of companies?

I am in favor, then, of seeing information gathered, analyzed, and disseminated, with the overall aim of providing and promoting studies of transnational business and its effects. I believe such work could well be tied in with that of the U.N. Nevertheless, I offer my basic support for this effort with certain qualifications.

First, it should be noted that transnational corporations already provide a great deal of information. Some of that information is required by law, but many companies, including the Shell companies, go far beyond what the law requires in disclosure of information. This information, freely made available, should first be examined carefully to determine how much and what kind of additional information is needed.

Second, the requirements governing disclosure of information to both the authorities and the public should not be discriminatory. Hence they should not apply only to companies forming part of an international grouping, but to all companies over a certain size. I am assuming that those responsible for this work would insist on proper analysis and would not be satisfied with mere generalizations. The frankness and openness shown all around indicates the willingness to view problems objectively. As I have already emphasized, the disclosure of information is all-important; it goes a long way toward counteracting criticism.

In the area of technical assistance and cooperation, some have suggested that U.N. personnel could advise local governments—especially negotiating teams dealing with transnational corporations. Another possibility that merits exploration is model contracts. Such proposals are in line with U.N. principles and practices, and expert advice is always helpful in engineering matters.

I myself have some doubts about whether outside legal experts and skilled negotiators are really needed. The governments with which the Shell companies have dealt have shown themselves to be more than capable of handling their side of the negotiations, whether on their own or with the expert assistance which is already available.

HARMONIZATION OF NATIONAL POLICIES

Taxation is the area in which harmony is most important. Investors would welcome an increased network of treaties concerning double taxation, and I think such treaties benefit both governments and investors.

That countries are in widely differing stages of development and have differing economic interests works against establishing a standard treaty which would be acceptable worldwide. Nevertheless, treaties should aim for a common treatment of such matters as dividends, interest, royalties, and capital profits. They should also provide for the negotiation of mutually acceptable price levels for transactions with companies operating in the other contracting state.

Also very important is the harmonization of environmental regulations, a process that must take into account the developmental differences between individual regions. Matters relating to conservation are greatly in need of international cooperation, a cooperation that must draw in the transnational corporations.

Another matter that might benefit from harmonization is the legislation on restrictive business practices. I believe that the method of controlling restrictive business practices could well vary from country to country, since it would have to depend on the country's level of economic development and on its social, economic, and political objectives.

GENERAL AGREEMENT ON TRANSNATIONAL CORPORATIONS

The issue here is the possibility and efficacy of an international agreement on transnational corporations to which governments could subscribe if they saw fit. Any government subscribing to such an agreement should uphold the principle of nondiscrimination: all companies over a certain size—and not just the transnational corporations—should be subject to the provisions.

I have some doubts, however, about whether governments would be willing to accept such a charter. In an address given in May 1973 to the International Chamber of Commerce, Dr. Manuel Peréz-Guerrero, the Director General of the United Nations Conference on Trade and Development, asked whether we will "see evolve one day an international code of conduct for transnational corporations," and said that this would "depend primarily on the ability of governments to adopt and enforce a coherent set of principles and regulations of universal application." I share the doubts implied in this statement, because I do not believe we can realistically expect the states to accept a code of conduct of binding legal obligations, or in certain circumstances to yield to an international organization their freedom to act against companies operating within their territory. They would regard such compliance as surrendering part of their sovereignty.

In the absence of agreement on a more general treaty containing binding legal obligations, the best that can realistically be achieved is the drawing-up of recommended guidelines—something that has already been done by the International Chamber of Commerce in their "Guidelines for International Investment." These guidelines provide the framework for further consideration and are also a useful means of identifying the problems related to international investment that arise for the home and host countries as well as for the investor.

Finally, it has been suggested that large groups of companies could be registered with an international organization under the auspices of the U.N.—an idea I support. Certain qualifying criteria would have to be established, and the companies that qualify would then have certain responsibilities, such as meeting minimum standards of disclosure and giving periodic reports. The companies so registered would also receive some privileges, such as access to procedures for complaint in cases of mistreatment.

The transnational corporations are leading the way down a road which all of us—governments and labor unions, developed and underdeveloped countries—see ahead. The openness that can result from a healthy exchange on the United Nations level would surely prove instructive and might well lead to better relationships. Such openness would show many people that international control will only be possible if the individual countries—and hence their governments—are willing to cooperate.

6: TRANSNATIONAL BUSINESS IN DEVELOPING COUNTRIES

DEVELOPMENT AS A DUTY

WHEN THE GOVERNMENT OF A COUNTRY ENTERS INTO negotiations with a transnational corporation, the objective is to reach agreement on a course of action that is mutually agreeable, with the understanding that each party will live up to its commitments. In some cases the initiative is taken by the transnational corporation, but it also happens quite often that government officials invite company representatives to meet with them to consider a deal.

International economic development is a vital, growing need. No country can stand on its own; even the strongest of countries is running a risk if it ignores other nations in its economic planning. This economic interdependence requires regional, international, and global trade and investment, transfer of know-how, easy communication, and unimpeded travel. In this discussion I am limiting myself to the developing countries, where the need is greatest, because in many respects they are inadequately equipped to cope with their problems.

Industrialized countries have a moral duty to help poorer countries develop economically. Yet more than duty is involved, because such aid also makes excellent economic and political sense, except to the short-sighted. Governments create the framework—unilaterally, bilaterally, and multilaterally—but the business community plays an enormous role in offering indispensable aid. But even with the best will in the world (which is exceedingly rare), it is not enough.

LONG-TERM INTERESTS

It is both inevitable and healthy for business to move abroad—hence the transnational corporation. That there should be such companies is no more surprising than that certain rivers flow through several countries.

Transnational corporations are not only the *instruments* of development but also the *result* of it. Although most of them (either privately or publicly owned) are based in the industrialized world, more and more of them are being established in the developing countries. The East-bloc countries are also creating transnational corporations.

We need no longer argue about whether transnational corporations should be allowed to exist and operate; rather, the question is, how we can best use them. This question becomes acutely important for a developing country that is negotiating with a transnational corporation. It is true that the governments of some developing countries are still poorly equipped and staffed and therefore need help in reaching a constructive agreement. I believe this can also be said of many of the transnational corporations, whose long-term interests are not served by a one-sided deal (*societas leonina*) that is unlikely to last. The government of a developing country has the option of retaining the services of private consultants. Another possibility is obtaining advice and help from international organizations such as the United Nations Center on Transnational Corporations, which can play a very useful role.

RISK AND RESPONSIBILITY

It is often assumed that in negotiations between transnational corporations and developing countries, the balance of power lies with business. The fact of the matter is that the corporation exposes itself to considerable risk, especially with regard to its investments. Adverse economic conditions may develop, and arbitrary political intervention may occur. Sometimes even the company's right to diplomatic representation is challenged. In this respect transnational corporations are at the mercy of the countries in which they conduct their business and make their investments.

Nevertheless, both parties to any negotiations have their strengths and weaknesses, and it is futile to argue about which enjoys the greater advantage. Both sides want a constructive and stable outcome in the interests of the people they represent.

Although a fundamental difference exists between the political responsibility of governments and the "commercial" responsibility of transnational corporations, it should be understood that the management of a company must be accountable and responsible, too—not only to governments, but also to its shareholders, creditors, trade unions, contractors, and suppliers. This includes people of many different nationalities, some of whom are citizens of developing countries. Together they represent the public at large—and few of them are "rich." Thus the suggestion that negotiations between governments and transnational corporations are essentially between self-seeking tycoons and socially motivated statesmen and civil servants is more than misguided; it is worse than a caricature. Representatives on both sides are serving a host of other people.

It bears repeating that the two parties have a common objective in their negotiations: they want a deal that will be mutually acceptable and beneficial. As in all negotiations, this requires being confident and following certain "rules of the game." In fact, the clearer and more constructive the rules, the greater the confidence of the parties involved.

PROTECTION FOR BUSINESS

As I have said before, prominent among these rules of the game is the law of the land. But it may be that in the early stages of a country's development the law is inadequate because it has not been written with modern social and economic developments in mind. Wherever this situation exists, however, legislators are at work to remedy it.

The activities of transnational corporations will naturally be governed by the sovereignty and laws of the countries in which they operate. But because a transnational corporation has both national and international aspects, the arrangement between such a corporation and the government will have to include some additional features on each side. The government might wish to know how the transnational corporation will "behave" in the field of labor relations, and the corporation will want certain assurances that will minimize the danger of arbitrary political decisions on the government's part.

When disputes occur, the transnational corporation will favor international arbitration through such agencies as the World Bank and the International Chamber of

Commerce. With due regard for the laws of the host countries, these agencies generally offer a more acceptable solution to the problem from the corporation's point of view.

TOWARD A CODE OF CONDUCT

It is true that "guidelines" or "principles" that set standards of behavior for transnational corporations provide nothing more than general direction. Nevertheless, they do make possible a clearer understanding of what is expected on all sides, thereby encouraging confidence and inspiring transnational business to grow and be effective.

Far from fighting such "encroachment" on its freedom, business has come to recognize the value of guidelines. In fact, the International Chamber of Commerce acted as a trailblazer when it adopted its "Guidelines for International Investment" in 1972. The Organization for Economic Co-operation and Development (OECD) followed in 1976 with its "Guidelines for Multinational Enterprises," and in 1977 the International Labour Organization (ILD) issued the "Tripartite Draft Declaration of Principles on Multinational Enterprises and Social Policy."

These are some of the most important efforts at formulating and encouraging universal high standards of behavior for transnational corporations—guidelines for business that also call for certain assurances from governments. Several other such documents are under discussion, the most comprehensive and ambitious of which is a project undertaken by the United Nations Commission on Transnational Corporations to develop a code of conduct.

I hope that the U.N. code will be practical and will

serve its principal purpose, which is to promote international economic and social development, especially in developing countries. Such promotion is of paramount importance, especially because business, for a variety of reasons, has found that it must now be much more selective in its transnational activities than it was in the 1950's and 1960's.

It would be very useful if future agreements between governments and transnational corporations made specific reference to accepted guidelines or principles, or to the relevant parts of documents in which guidelines and principles are spelled out. This would have several advantages: 1) there would be a clearer understanding of the commitments being made; 2) the possibility of future arguments would be reduced; 3) the practical significance of widely accepted codes of conduct would be underscored; and 4) the implications of such codes could be tested in practice.

If a proposal to incorporate references to existing codes of conduct or sets of guidelines meant that certain parties could not reach an agreement, this would be most regrettable. However, it would still be better than the other possible result: a later falling-out when the two parties discovered that the implications of an agreement were not completely clear to them.

Rights and duties and appropriate mechanisms for the settlement of disputes should be clearly spelled out as an integral part of any deal. This will promote confidence on both sides, confidence that will encourage development.

OUTLOOK FOR THE FUTURE

What we need most is greater understanding between foreign investors, the governments of host countries, and the home governments. Better understanding would lead to increased confidence and a strengthening of relationships.

The first line of advance is reassessment of the roles of investor, host government, and home government. The foreign investor has already learned that he has everything to gain by helping to develop the prosperity of the host country. In a modern market economy, the business firm is not apart from or in conflict with society; it flourishes only when it clearly contributes to the interests of society.

At the same time, it must be recognized that a number of people have genuine fears about foreign investment. Some of the fears are unjustified, because they are rooted in an underestimation of the power of national sovereignty and an overestimation of the power of transnational companies. It is important that companies do what they can to dispel such fears by providing more information that is easily accessible. Moreover, governments should strive to better understand both the nature of the problem and their own strength.

The growth of international business has coincided with a period of progressive political development, as is shown by the growth in number and importance of nation-states, and by the strengthening of the international community of states. Hence there has been a growth in both independence and interdependence, which has produced a conflict that has not yet been completely resolved. I believe this is one of the principal reasons for the tensions in international economic relationships.

These tensions are apparent in the attitudes some governments take toward international investment. They fear that joining a system of international economic interdependence, as is characteristic of the world economy, may endanger national economic independence—a dilemma that lies at the very heart of the matter. Nonetheless, it is worth noting that government-owned companies are today playing a growing role in the ranks of the transnational corporations. We are also beginning to see transnational corporations based in developing countries.

These facts underscore the need for deepening our understanding. We are caught up in a period of tremendous change, and our ability to adapt to change will determine our future success. Charges and counter-charges lead nowhere; our basic assumptions must be reviewed.

One false assumption is that the developing regions of the world will always remain underdeveloped. New evidence on world trade shows that the productivity of developing countries is greatly increasing. Today they are exporting a much greater volume of goods than they exported in the past. The more these countries advance, the greater the diversification of the international economy, which will in turn bring about new relationships and patterns in international economic cooperation.

Our willingness to consider the problems of transnational corporations under the auspices of the U.N. will serve as a healthy reminder that we should seek solutions to such problems through international discussion and joint measures. I have every confidence that many of the problems we now face in international business can be resolved.

PART III

THE
RESPONSE
OF BUSINESS

7: REFLECTIONS ON BUSINESS AND THE ENVIRONMENT

THE QUALITY OF LIFE

INDUSTRIALIZATION HAS CONFERRED A GREAT MANY benefits on our society, but we don't hear much about them lately. Although unemployment is currently a problem, the amount of work which industrialization has managed to create is not to be taken lightly. Overall, we enjoy great material prosperity. Workers today have a much shorter workweek than did previous generations. They have more free time, and they also have the money to do something useful and pleasant with that time.

Think especially of the *mobility* that our industrialized prosperity has brought us. A vacation is no longer a trip to a local beach: we travel to faraway parts of our own country, and even go overseas. Virtually every family owns a car, which by itself brings about a definite increase in mobility. People who live in crowded cities treasure the opportunity to take a drive in the country.

But these changes have their drawbacks—unpleasant things that are now drawing increasing attention. In some parts of the world, too many people live on too little land. The result is tension, aggressive attitudes, and heightened dangers in traffic. In addition, many people working in industry complain about monotony in their work and life. We also hear charges about the monotonous design of the homes and buildings shooting up on the edges of our cities.

The various complaints about urban life—about modern education and so forth—combined with the enormous technical improvements in our communications network have led to new or increased confusion in many areas. Most people do not understand technology, and therefore tend to view it as an enemy. New patterns of organization and new machines, the fruit of technology, have changed and disturbed the traditional patterns of personal relationships.

And when we look at these factors, we must also consider pollution. Not only are water, air, and earth being polluted, but our ears are being polluted by increasing noise. Clearly, the quality of our life is being affected. At the same time we can say that we have never had it so good: when it comes to food, shelter, transportation, clothing, health care, free time, and entertainment, we have more than previous generations ever dreamed of. Nevertheless, it appears that we are becoming more and more unhappy—at least, if we believe what certain commentators and social critics say. We would do well to think about these things together, for they involve all of us, whether actively or passively, whether for better or for worse, whether we are the perpetrators of these problems or merely their victims.

Physical Problems
What I mean to say about business and the environment is not new, but it needs saying nonetheless, because certain persistent misunderstandings must be cleared away. The relation between business and the environment is an intensely relevant and timely topic for discussion. Because

business in its many forms is an integral part of society, the question of the environment cannot be considered apart from the place of business in modern life.

In our time, businesses (especially industries) have grown in size and number—a growth that has no parallel in previous history. Hence business is scrutinized today as never before, and it plays a major role in those environmental questions that are talked about today and strike fear in our hearts tomorrow. But this does not mean that the problem of environmental imbalance has been caused exclusively—or even primarily—by business. It is not fair to think immediately and only of industry when someone mentions environmental concern; many other sectors of society should also come to mind. Agriculture, recreation, the cities—those great concentrations of people with all they consume and produce—and transportation by road, river, sea, and air all have significant effects on the environment.

Business and industry are indeed part of the picture, but they are not the whole problem—or even the biggest part of the problem. Nevertheless, industry should be ready to say, "Yes, we are part of the problem. We have great responsibilities in this area, and we have much to learn. We started some projects twenty years ago without being properly aware of the environmental consequences, so there are some things that we are obliged to set right."

If such an outlook took hold and business was willing to talk about its environmental responsibilities, we would make more advances—and without polarization. But the larger question still remains: how does society in general make use of nature? Man uses nature to improve his lot, but sometimes the ultimate effect is that he worsens his condition. Man in his environment—that is the great issue before us.

Freedom and Social Concerns

I have put man before the environment because man is indeed central. I believe that his welfare has to take priority over that of plants, animals, water, land, and air. The other creatures and elements of nature exist for man's use—and it is precisely for this reason that they should not be abused.

I am presupposing here that individual freedom must be subordinate to the greater interests of the community. I do not mean to denigrate man's fundamental right to personal freedom; in fact, I believe that this right must be defended by all reasonable means. But this right is necessarily limited by the rights of others. The question of exactly where this limit lies is as old as society itself; it is the question of Cain and Abel, or, to use modern language, the question of freedom versus social limitation.

Social limitations also play a role in environmental problems. Who is to set the limits? Who is to make certain that they are respected? Implicit here are such issues as the individual and society, the citizen and government, and law and authority and power. It is not enough to offer a general theory, because we must also be able to give an answer in specific situations.

The greatest stumbling block here is that we human beings, despite all our good intentions, are egoistic and short-sighted. If we narrowly assign the task of determining the limit between freedom and social obligation to an individual or an institution, it is not likely that the two will be reasonably balanced.

As long as industry threatens the welfare of the environment, the question of environmental protection cannot be left exclusively to industry itself. With no outside consultation and control, industry's own environmental concern would in many cases be too limited. A balance must be established in which all aspects of the environment are properly emphasized, and the market mechanism cannot achieve this alone.

THE ENVIRONMENTAL CHALLENGE

I have already indicated that business cannot tackle the challenge of environmental protection on its own; it must consult with other sectors of society and cooperate with them in order to achieve the desired balance. But I do want to point out that the very first source of environmental protection lies within business itself—that is, within areas with which the business has direct contact. Public attention invariably focuses on the things that go wrong or are threatening to go wrong, and this is as it should be, but all too often we forget how much business itself is doing for the environment.

Generally speaking, businesses are managed by well-meaning people who are responsible citizens concerned about the welfare of society. Moreover, businessmen generally have a keen perception of what they are doing and causing to be done. With this outlook—a healthy attitude based on solid knowledge—businessmen will for the most part act in the interests of the environment. Yet, important as this is, it is not enough. It is not only that well-meaning and capable people can fail: we must also remember that the cumulative effect of acceptable encroachments on the environment may well turn out to be unacceptable.

I believe that in this area there is no difference between private business and government-owned business. The environmental problems are the same for both; it cannot be said that the one type of business is easier on the environment than the other in comparable circumstances. A similar observation can be made when we compare the environmental impact of the decisions made by the public authorities with the environmental impact of decisions made by private business. It simply cannot be argued that government has a better "track record" than business.

Unforeseen Consequences

To some extent, all of us have underestimated the consequences of rapid industrialization. We welcomed industrialization because of the prosperity it brought, but we were not sufficiently aware of some of its negative by-products. One of the physical by-products was the effect on the environment, something we will have to pay much more attention to in the future. But we must not forget that we were right to welcome industrialization joyfully, and that we should continue to think positively about business and industry.

Neither government nor business was able to foresee all the results of industrialization. In earlier generations government was not equipped to deal with these matters in an efficient manner or with proper insight. We are not constitutionally organized to cope with the problems posed by modern industry. Certainly some streamlining will have to take place, but the changes that are needed cannot occur overnight. Often the government's left hand does not know what its right hand is doing; the philosophies of the various governmental branches and departments are frequently in conflict. I do not mean this comment as a reproach; it simply illustrates my point that our industrial development has been so rapid that the insight and apparatus needed for proper supervision is lagging far behind.

Consultation and Cooperation

It is our task, then, to improve this situation. Business, with its environmental problems, will need government, and vice versa. Despite its decisive political power, government is no more able than industry to solve the problem alone.

It would be so convenient if mere prohibition would suffice, if the government could simply say, "Such-and-such is not allowed," and that would be the end of it. Often the technology to solve the problem is available, but every intervention leads to fresh consequences. What we need is a harmonious, unified approach that will be implemented as a package. In any event, simple prohibitions are too exclusively negative to be truly effective.

Business, after all, is an active part of society through which many are served; it is not the hobby of a limited group of people looking out only for their own interests. Thus business must be given a chance to do what is right in a manner that it finds acceptable. If it doesn't get that chance, it cannot continue to exist. What consequences the collapse of business would produce we see foreshadowed every time a business halts its operations or even announces plans to cut back.

If a balanced program for protecting the environment is to be created, business and government must consult with each other. Criticism alone, however useful and necessary, cannot solve the problem. It is especially important that we as individuals put our shoulders to the wheel, for unless the average person starts to learn self-discipline, and is educated about the problem, the battle is lost.

Sacrifices and Environmental Costs

The great environmental problems we face can be solved in a reasonable way only if many people are willing to make sacrifices—not just certain groups here and there, but people in all of society. To some extent, the needed sacrifices are already being made. Various projects have been launched—though not simply for environmental reasons; they have seemed economically attractive as well. Of course, the actual fact of the matter is that such projects are becoming economically unattractive because of pollution control costs. And certain promising projects are not being implemented simply because the environment would be harmed. These are incidental decisions, but they are certainly difficult enough to make. In any case, we should recognize that such cases indeed involve a form of economic sacrifice.

Particularly difficult are the physical problems caused by our innovations. One such problem is the environmental cost of our transportation system. Sometimes environmentalists suggest that we should give up our cars, but are we prepared to take such a step? Could we ever be persuaded to do so? And if we did, think of the economic consequences of a drastic slowdown in the automobile industry, with all the unemployment that would result in related industries and in communities dependent on the industry for most of their employment.

An even greater difficulty is all the chemical poison we use to fight insects and weeds. Yet we also know that, as the world population has increased over the last fifty years, we would have had no hope of feeding all the hungry mouths if chemical pesticides had *not* been used. And despite their use, food is in such short supply in many countries today that people are starving by the thousands. Certainly some chemicals are dangerous, but banning all of them would exacerbate the world's food problem. How, then, are we to strike a balance?

Toward International Solutions
Through these two examples we can already see that national environmental problems call for international solutions. Transportation problems have international ramifications; many of the rivers being polluted by our poisons and chemical pesticides flow through more than one country. And we all share in the responsibility for the oceans and the atmosphere.

Fortunately, many environmental advances have been made under the auspices of the United Nations. Significant regional progress is evident, and international discussion concerning the proper use of the sea has been going on for some time.

Because it is active in various countries, business has a special role to play here. Through the exchange of information and the transfer of technological capacities, businesses are often in a position to act more quickly than governments. They can assist governments in both word and deed. When businesspeople sometimes forget this, we hear complaints that the transnational corporations are dodging the regulations established to protect the environment. Unfortunately, there will always be people who disregard regulations, but such misconduct is the exception rather than the rule.

Reflection on Priorities

We must begin by tackling these problems at home. What are our national priorities? What do we really want— higher industrial production or cleaner air, industry or agriculture, tourism or no tourism? A little of both, I suppose. We face complicated issues that require careful thought—and no indictment of the past. It does no good to reproach a government of a hundred years ago for not having foreseen the problems that would develop late in the twentieth century.

Fortunately, our democratic institutions allow for responsible discussion, although some streamlining needs to be done in this area, as I have indicated. And it is important that business be involved in the discussion. Naturally, the government has the last word, but business can be more helpful as an advisor and a participant than as merely the recipient of regulations.

The third participant in this discussion should be universities. A university offers both knowledgeable people and the capacity to conduct research. Moreover, it has direct contact with young people, who have their own contribution to make to the discussions about the environment.

We must learn to handle our affairs better. To the extent that we are successful, we will reduce the arguments that have been exacerbated in recent years, arguments between the young and the old, the university and the government, the university and business, and so forth.

Business, then, has an obligation to help government make wise decisions about the environment, decisions which it must help to implement. It must do as much as it can to bring healing and prevent further deterioration. At the same time, we should not forget that the rights and obligations of business are limited, just as its capacities are limited; and the public authorities have the last word. Still, the legislative and executive officials have an obligation to consider all the quantifiable—and even the unquantifiable—aspects of the problem as they make political decisions. These decisions will call for more and more sacrifices on the part of many, sacrifices which we must regard as the price to be paid for progress.

Are our societal and governmental structures adequate to deal with environmental questions? I firmly believe that they are. Organizations will evolve and administrative regulations will have to be improved, but nothing in the argument I have presented suggests that a fundamental change in our society is needed. We must face the future with a commitment to cooperation and genuinely open discussion. This involves thinkers and doers, government and citizenry, society and business.

8: ETHICS AND BUSINESS

MISCONCEPTIONS

ON A RECENT SUNDAY MORNING, ONE OF MY FRIENDS nearly walked out of church because he was deeply offended by what he heard proclaimed from the pulpit. The preacher, using unambiguous language, had explained that greed is the engine that drives business, and that the large transnational business, in particular, furthers social injustice. My friend had heard such talk before in church, but the words of the preacher that Sunday morning were the straw that broke the camel's back. The next day he went to visit the minister, a man of deep convictions and a strong sense of calling. They had a frank discussion in which it became clear that the preacher had only a vague sense of what goes on in the business world and what motivates businesspeople.

In our society many people are still ignorant about how a big business operates, and many misconceptions hang in the air. Yet I must admit that we as businesspeople are largely to blame for the lack of good information that would counter such ideas. We must properly prepare ourselves for the tremendous amount of work waiting to be done in this area if we want to fulfill our obligations in a more systematic and rational manner than we have in the past. I do not expect that we will make ourselves popular, but we must certainly work harder at fostering an understanding of what we do and fail to do.

I would like to focus particularly on the measure in which businesses in general, and large companies in particular, are bound to social norms and moral criteria. Certainly no well-meaning person would deny that anyone, whatever his or her line of work, must maintain moral standards, and that we all bear a certain responsibility toward society. But what are the practical implications of believing this to be true? To what extent do such rules for conduct apply to a business?

INDIVIDUAL RESPONSIBILITY

To answer this question, we must concentrate on the ethics of the individual in the context of business. In addition to following societal rules, an organization must follow its own prescribed and applied rules. And people in business are personally responsible for their behavior, for ensuring that their conduct satisfies ethical norms. They must make sure that the organization as a whole acts in a socially acceptable manner.

In business there is, in fact, a gradation of responsibilities. The higher level businesspeople are more responsible for the ethical and social aspects of business. The directors of a business try to balance against each other the interests of the employees, the shareholders, and society. What is demanded of them in addition to proper conduct and concern for the individual is that they meet the needs of their customers or clients in an efficient and profitable way, thereby seeking to match their competition. If you to asked me to formulate a businessman's oath, I would come up with something like this: "In the domain of trade, agriculture, or industry in the broadest sense, I will offer a service to others while keeping the interests of the owners and employees of the company in mind, using profit as a stimulus and a measure of service."

As I mentioned earlier, profit is indispensable to progress. It provides the capital that is necessary to finance economic growth, and it assures the owners of the business—that is, the shareholders—a return on their investment. Without profit a company is not in a position to provide adequately for the needs of its employees and to wisely use its resources. On the one hand the profit criterion appeals to a typical human inclination; on the other hand it helps to prevent any waste of human labor and resources. Thus it is a motive for the individual as well as an economic barometer.

I am talking here about businesses that operate in a competitive sphere, like those in a mixed economy. I am opposed to monopolies: no business, whether private or public, should be allowed to engage in monopolistic practices. It is the task of the government to see to it that this rule is followed, because when it is violated, society pays the price.

Now that I have alluded to "public" business, I should go on to observe that for certain practical reasons I prefer private business to government-owned business. I see a place for the latter only in those instances in which private business proves impossible. Unless a public business is told that it must operate just like a private business (which, for political reasons, is often difficult, if not impossible), it will be inclined to assume a monopolistic position, operate on government subsidies, or be generally uneconomical.

RESPONSIBILITY OF
DIRECTORS AND MANAGERS

Business—both large and small—is an especially useful element in modern society. Thus business is not to be thought of as simply a means to achieve personal gain, without any thought of social responsibility. Certainly some economic factors stimulate socially responsible conduct, but there is more to the picture. Of fundamental importance is the conduct and attitude of businesspeople, especially that of directors and managers.

The directors and managers are ordinary people who have differing views of life. Many are Christians and try to live according to Christian principles. In business circles, the percentage of people who take their responsibilities seriously is as high as anywhere else. But because businesspeople are ordinary people, the "conduct" of business cannot be exclusively determined by their social consciousness and economic wishes. There must be supervision and review from the outside, and there is—plenty of it. Business is subject to local laws, has to respond to the demands of labor unions, and must contend with the mass media and public opinion. It is also subject to external controls and supervision via business councils and bodies established by business itself.

The directors and managers of a business simply cannot afford to keep silent when facing the world; they must make clear the social task of business. In a balanced way they must also try to meet the constant demands coming from all directions, in the process serving the interests of all—not just those of one person or one group.

SOCIAL RESPONSIBILITY

Social responsibility involves obligations toward consumers, employers, shareholders, the environment, and society in general. Although I have already touched on these aspects, I want to make a few more remarks here. In delineating our responsibilities toward society, it might be useful to consider the recommendations made by the Economic and Social Council of the United Nations.

In a statement which I offered as a contribution to the report, I declared that transnational business should be structured in as open a manner as possible, and that transnational businesses ought to keep the public informed about their activities and plans, except when this proves impossible for reasons of competition.

I also support without reservation the recommendation that governments provide greater aid for international development. I believe that such aid should be directed especially toward alleviating the needs of the poorest in the developing countries. This is in no way to deny that international economic activity must also continue to contribute to development—and in growing measure.) Related to this emphasis is a recommendation that the governments of the countries in which the transnationals have their headquarters must not hinder these companies from transferring to developing countries certain labor-intensive production processes involving unskilled workers. I fully support this recommendation, including the part that stipulates that the employees in the home country who are put out of work by these measures should receive assistance from their government so that they can be retrained and put to work elsewhere.

I also support the recommendations about international norms for industrial safety and concern for worker's health, but with the understanding that they have to be practically applied to specific situations in each country. The various governments would then have to reserve the power, in cooperation with the International Labor Organization and the World Health Organization, to apply those norms to their own circumstances.

ENVIRONMENTAL RESPONSIBILITY

Businesses, especially the larger ones, stand exposed to much criticism because they pollute the environment as they provide society with the goods and services it needs. It does sometimes happen that the products and procedures used by business are harmful to the environment at a certain stage, perhaps during the manufacturing process or during transportation and distribution—or perhaps during consumption.

Complicated problems face us here. If we are to solve them, we must not only have a well-developed sense of social responsibility and put extra effort into technological research, but society must also make some difficult decisions, decisions in which a balance is struck between maintaining reasonable costs and keeping the environment pure. In the last chapter we considered these problems more fully, yet this issue is so important that a few points bear repeating.

First and foremost, the businesses involved must strictly follow the law. But in these cases in which the law does not conclusively address the problem that arises, businesses—especially large businesses—are obliged to take the lead in determining a viable soultion. The rule to be remembered here is an old and reliable one: "An ounce of prevention is worth a pound of cure." In other words, businesses may not simply limit themselves to obeying existing regulations. We must recognize possible threats to the environment in good time, and take steps to conserve and protect it whenever possible.

We must develop new structures and methods so that the environment will not be taxed, or will at least be burdened as little as possible. Scientific research must lead the way here.

TOWARD GREATER UNDERSTANDING

It is urgently important that society gain clearer general insight into the role of business, especially businesses that are active on the international scene and operate in more than one country.

In this time of almost explosive economic and social developments, businesses must pursue their socioeconomic goals with the means available in a world that is flawed, politically and otherwise. Sovereign states—and there are many more of them in the post-colonial era— find themselves confronted with international economic expansion brought about by peace and technical progress. The enormous amount of work being undertaken by the International Chamber of Commerce is one of the many indications of the willingness of business to face the problems spawned by these developments. This cooperation does not arise simply from a desire to maintain friendly relations, but stems especially from an awareness of the absolute necessity of clearing away fundamental misunderstandings which could have particularly damaging consequences.

It should not be forgotten that big businesses, which are the most important targets of the critics, are the property of a large public. They belong not to a few "rich" people or to "them," but to "us." The actual ownership of the shares of stock has become very diversified through institutional investors such as pension-fund trustees, trust companies, and insurance companies. Millions of people have become direct or indirect co-owners of large companies, although many of them are not even aware of this fact.

We think it normal—and rightly so—that people with a little spare money receive interest when they deposit their money in a bank account. Then why should we deny a business the right to stand up for the interests of its shareholders? Are people forgetting what generates the interest that the bank pays? Why should we be so concerned about wages and employment opportunities but unconcerned about the value of shares of stock, the dividends paid to stockholders, and the continued existence of the businesses in which they hold stock? All these aspects of business are socioeconomically important, and thus we must include them all in our consideration of business ethics.

I have little appreciation for so-called social visions which are only partly based on reality. Those who bear practical responsibilities and are obliged to do more than talk must examine the full picture and then act accordingly. And from time to time they must publicly emphasize the importance of keeping the entire picture in mind.

9: BUSINESS IN A CHANGING WORLD

UNDERSTANDING HISTORY

IT IS NOT EASY TO UNDERSTAND HISTORY, ESPE-cially when we focus on social change. This topic involves great numbers of historians, sociologists, economists, social geographers, demographers, political scientists, theologians, statisticians, and philosophers. Every area studied produces uncertainty and differing opinions; consequently, the clearest and most important changes are universally recognized.

Let me give you an example. We know quite precisely where, how, and to what extent slavery was practiced in the so-called Christian West, but how our ancestors were able to justify slavery to themselves and how they could live with it for so long remains an intriguing riddle.

SOCIAL DEVELOPMENTS

It is even more difficult to gain insight into the way in which modern social developments take place. If we look, for example, at the place of youth in our society and note how completely different it is from the place of youth during earlier generations, we cannot help but wonder how this shift will alter the patterns of our society. We also wonder how women's changing roles will affect social patterns.

A totally different aspect comes to the fore when we

examine the potential significance of the anonymous shareholder. What is his or her future? How are we to properly understand the role of the institutional investor—not just statistically but socially and economically? How many of our good citizens ever stop to think that they own part of a number of companies, that they are actually shareholders and therefore members of a group which some people think of contemptuously? What will be the outcome of all of the changes in relationships of authority? Where is the growing secularization headed? And what about the future role of the church? Finally, can we properly foresee the consequences—not only physical but social—of our greatly increased mobility?

Commenting on "the new dependencies," Professor J. J. A. Van Doorn observed recently:

> We face problems which we do not even know how to describe properly, problems which we are not even able to arrange in a global order of importance. The massive quantity of information reaching us daily is insufficient. On the contrary, it appears that it is precisely the great quantity of the information in our hands that is obscuring our vision.

FUTURE CHANGES

Things become completely impossible when we try to gain insight into future changes. If we do not know the past well, if we do not understand the present, if the change in our society is governed by some sort of Mendel's law, how can we possibly understand what is to come?

Our planners are certainly useful people, and I am not proposing to deprive them of their livelihood. Neither am I suggesting that the futurologists should stop trying to simulate future conditions and situations. My point is simply that the best they can give us is *possible* future developments. Their projections are never fully translated into reality—unlike parts of economic life, they cannot somehow be measured by clever people, or be calculated for the future. They simply cannot tell us what tomorrow's world will look like.

As long as we recognize this fact, we don't have much reason to be uneasy. If we are disappointed, it is only because not much has changed in this area of prediction, apart from the fact that computers have replaced the intestines of slaughtered animals. The life's work of Herman Kahn illustrates the point. His studies are based on the conviction that we can make quite a few predictions about the future, a belief that I am not prepared to share. He and his colleagues at the Hudson Institute speak in global terms once they are done with all their philosophizing and quantifying, yet even their prognoses recognize the likelihood of great variations. No concrete policies can be built on such uncertain projections, and people in the world of praxis still rely on policies.

But we know that society has always been in a state of change, and that we are always on the way to something different. We also know that it is our responsibility to exert some influence over the changes taking place both around us and in us.

INTERDEPENDENCE AND INTERRELATION

What do we need in order to carry out our responsibilities? Society has grown, and it is becoming increasingly clear that no part of society is independant from the others, that every change has some significance and causes a chain reaction, either visible or invisible.

The unbridled instant publicity that we must learn to live with plays a dominant role in all of this. Everyone now has his or her own soapbox, and we are all looking over each other's shoulders. It is a simple matter to be a demagogue. Action groups are social forces to be reckoned with; they reproduce easily and manage to function and wield power without much difficulty. The effects of these changes can be either good or bad. The negative consequence is that nothing is safe from attack anymore, and it does seem easier to achieve negative results than positive, constructive ones.

Thus, in all sorts of socially important areas, our responsibility is much greater today than it was in earlier eras. We must be judicious in what we do and say, as well as in what we *don't* do and say. This awareness ought to shape our attitude and approach, whether we are thinkers, talkers, or doers. Unfortunately, many of us fall short in this respect—a point of that is made often, but is sufficiently important to merit repeating.

THE SOCIALIZATION OF SOCIETY

This may strike you as a puzzling expression, and it is indeed tautological, but it is clear nevertheless. What it means is that individuals and groups—those who bear the responsibility for one facet of society, however limited—must be increasingly conscious of belonging to the greater whole which we call society. This change in sensibility has dual consequences: it affects both their actions and their response to the actions of others. Let's look at some examples.

There was a time when we could walk or ride on the left-hand side of the road, or cross the street anywhere without worrying. To do so today would be to endanger ourselves and others. Therefore children (and even adults) are given formal instruction in pedestrian safety. The pollution problem of the Rhine, which winds through several countries, has made us painfully aware that pollution in one place can endanger the health of many people who live elsewhere. Conditions in Rotterdam's harbor concern all of Western Europe. Developments in country A often have direct consequences for country B. A strong currency is a good thing in itself, but it can have negative effects that touch everyone in the country, either directly or indirectly.

Such connections are to be found everywhere in economic, social, and political life, on both the national and the international level. And connections exist not only within the spheres of economic, social, and political life, but also between them. This network of relationships makes us wonder exactly where we draw the boundaries between economics, society, and politics.

This complexity also leads to the demand that everyone in a position of responsibility think, investigate, and learn a great deal more. Our vulnerability has not only increased the number of people in our society who bear responsibility, but has also increased the extent of that responsibility in many cases. The penalty for failure is now much greater—and yet we must act. I wish that people who watch events from a safe distance could develop some sense of the pressure that the bearers of responsibility feel.

I believe that the greatest change our generation has experienced has been triggered by the increasing interrelation and interdependence of people and things, and the growing insight into the coherence of the system, however imperfect—changes that will surely influence the future. We have all become more socially responsible, and we are being reminded of this ever more directly and clearly. Unfortunately, the appeal for social responsibility or the demand for solidarity (I am using these two terms interchangeably, even though they do not have exactly the same meaning) has also been misused. But, given our communications technology and our guarantees of freedom of opinion, such misuse cannot be entirely avoided.

NEW EMPHASES

Naturally, the obligation to keep society in mind as we act is not new. In the West, the Christian ethic is centuries old. What is new is the emphasis this obligation is now receiving, and the extent to which it is now considered to apply to practical politics as well as the private sphere. And where this change has not yet occurred, it is at least being advocated. Our religious and ethical responsibilities are being confirmed and increased by social and technological developments to which we simply cannot close our eyes, regardless of what we might wish to do.

Let me give you a couple of illustrations. In the Netherlands we have a Foundation for Bio-sciences and Society. The existence of such an institution clearly testifies to the social responsibility expected of practitioners of the newer sciences. And a series of writings in legal theory on the theme "Justice and Society" is hailed as being particularly relevant today, a response that clearly suggests that in an earlier era the connection between justice and society was not so close, or was not perceived as being close. The purpose of this series of writings is to get away from the notion of law and justice as an "independent phenomenon," which seems to me to be a good way of stating the issue. We even talk about the socialization of government. And the question of church and state, though as old as the struggle between the pope and the emperor, is today being discussed within the framework of social responsibility.

My point is also illustrated by the position of the modern university. According to a newspaper report, Dr. J. A. van Kemenade declared recently: "It is of great importance to the future of the university that it be aware of its social responsibility. As I see it, this awareness must be the foundation for a further reformation of research, instruction and administration." Van Kemenade argued that the social function of the university has become too peripheral a matter. Not much progress has been made in the socialization of science, even though it was once made an explicit goal.

Let me give you one final example. The Foundation for Society and Business gathers facts and opinions about developments in society and business, and the influence they have upon each other. Again, this is nothing new, but one or two generations ago very few people would have seen the need or usefulness of such an institution.

If you are the type of person who is satisfied with the status quo, you are probably alarmed at this point. You sense that I am getting into political questions here, and you are right: social questions simply cannot be discussed without getting into politics. But I do not intend my remarks to favor a particular political party.

IMPLICATIONS FOR BUSINESS

When one thinks of the social emphasis in business, one is immediately reminded of the employees. This is entirely correct, for apart from one-man companies, all businesses are work communities that depend on internal solidarity. But the relationships among co-workers have a broader impact as well: they affect society.

Defining this solidarity may incline the man in the street—and often the politician as well—to think in terms of a company's obligations toward its employees. This is as it should be, but when we are talking about the social aspect (even when considering only the company's internal structure), it is not enough to talk about the relationships between managers and employees; the relationships of the workers themselves are also important. Solidarity must occur on every level, both horizontally and vertically, and managers are most responsible for encouraging and developing it.

As we now look beyond the inner workings of the company, we must turn to the clients or customers. Also to be considered is the owner or the group of owners—the shareholders—who together own the business. Since each is, obviously, a member of society, he has certain social rights and obligations, just as we all do. How are we to view this from a social point of view? What are the rights and obligations involved? Do social priorities exist in this context?

Business as a Social Phenomenon
I believe we must begin with society. All too often it is forgotten that a business is a goal-oriented work community in which making products or services available is central. In this sense business is a social phenomenon.

In order to realize the social goals it sets for itself, a business needs workers with various capabilities and responsibilities, and it needs finances—in other words, it needs employees and providers of capital who will work together to create a goal-directed organization. Each group has rights and obligations of its own. (In some cases, of course, labor and capital come from the same source.) And together, labor and providers of capital are socially obligated to act in a generally acceptable way as they produce desired goods or make available appreciated services.

As I see it, striving for this goal is the real social priority, and the responsibility involved cannot be placed solely on the shoulders of the employer and manager. (After all, in any except the smallest of modern businesses, the manager or director is himself an employee.) The responsibility must be shared by all who are involved in the business, even if different roles and responsibilities are assigned to different individuals and categories of employees. If we truly regard social responsibility as a universal demand (and I do believe that we should regard it as such), and if we think not exclusively of our own interests but of the interests of our group, we cannot help but draw this conclusion.

Naturally, this involves a framework established by the government, a framework that makes it possible for the various obligations, rights, and interests of all concerned to come into their own. Such a framework will keep the business on the proper track.

Social Interests
This starting point has consequences for many problems found in business, both internal and external. Both the

workers and those who provide the capital must keep social interests in mind and, in the final analysis, subject themselves to them. But how are social interests to be measured? No absolute yardstick exists, but I would certainly point to the market as an important criterion.

The role of the market is not absolute, and we are not to look to it as the source of all good. Yet practice reveals that the market can be violated only temporarily or to a limited extent—at least in a system that wishes to take all social factors into account. Even the leaders of OPEC, which is the biggest cartel in world history, are beginning to realize this.

I do not mean to say that a violation of the market can never be justified; on the contrary, social matters may sometimes require it. Yet such situations are exceptions, and the burden of proof always lies with those who propose to deviate from the market. The alternative—that is, excluding market considerations as a matter of principle—has dangerous political, social, and economic implications, as can be illustrated by what goes on in communist countries.

It is a shame that we are still supporting a one-sided conception of the business enterprise as an economic phenomenon when the social aspects are getting increasing recognition, even from arch-conservatives. The economic conception of business is correct, but it is too limited. Those discussing and reporting on business are now making more attempts to bring its social side into the picture—a change symptomatic of changing attitudes about business.

It is by no means easy to take the wind out of the sails of political critics, concerned religious figures, labor unions, and professional commentators. What we must begin with is the insight that economic action should be assessed in terms of its social significance—something easier said than done.

If we limit ourselves to the corporate annual report, we see that it is already difficult enough, in this time of inflation, fluctuating currencies, and antiquated fiscal systems, to understand the meaning of balance sheets and methods of calculating profits and losses; but it is even more difficult to write a truly satisfying "social report." There are simply too many matters that cannot be quantified, too many words that do not indicate precisely what is meant, and too many contexts and relations that cannot be properly analyzed. But many modern businesses and their advisors, including both national and international companies, are working on these problems, a development that I find encouraging.

I do not think our goal should be two separate reports—one report for economic matters and one for social implications. Because the social and economic aspects of business are inseparable, we should strive to develop a single, unified report.

No Place for Private Business?

My theme is change, and one question that arises is what change means for private business. We are faced with an enormously difficult task—adapting to current social, economic, and political changes—and the struggle will prove too much for many people.

But the biggest problem—indeed, danger—is the idea, accepted by many people, that private business has no future because it no longer has any right to exist or will no longer be given a chance. Here I am not thinking primarily of those who leave no room for private business in their political philosophy; a much greater threat, as I see it, is that so many people are going along with the current trend simply out of a complete lack of insight. These are the people who are all too easily influenced by one idea or another.

All those who are not aware of the great usefulness of private business are liable to oppose it—and not only because they concentrate exclusively on the economic side of business. If this attitude stems from ignorance about the valuable social role business plays, it can be changed, because a careful analysis will reveal the contribution that business does in fact make.

No person or group in our society may claim a monopoly on social concern and involvement—not even the people who do the most talking about social needs. Business must be conscious of its many-sided responsibility, but it must also demand that its great social contribution be recognized. If the general public would develop this concept about business, we would not need to worry about the future of private business.

I do not envy politicians. They must continually discuss and make decisions about a growing—and increasingly complicated—range of matters about which they have little knowledge. The same can be said about the bureaucrats, the communications people, the professors, and various other groups, though I am not making this point to suggest that such people lack dedication and ability.

Business Participation

To reduce the difficulty of determining what is and is not in the social interest (for this is indeed the issue at stake), we can do a number of things. Since I am dealing here with business and its place in society, I will mention only the desirability of a policy that would require the active participation of businesses, and that would provide information and insight about business to politicians, civil servants, and teachers in all institutions. This should not be made a priority only when special problems crop up; it should be the usual program that business actively implements.

I remember a politician who was very impressed when he visited a large natural science laboratory owned by a private business. Afterward he remarked, "What struck me the most is that the people who work in the laboratory think in just the same way we do." What in the world was he thinking before he made the visit? Naturally, his hosts must also have gained some insight into what motivates this man and his colleagues in the political arena.

I am not making a proposal for a more active program of "public relations"; what I am promoting is that the business world develop an entirely different attitude. What we must realize is that the interconnected systems have become so big, the opportunities for misunderstanding so enormous, and the social consequences often so unforeseeable that those who bear responsibility must be much better informed than they were before. They must also make themselves better understood, an area in which it would not be difficult to improve. If each person were to think about his or her area of expertise and take some initiative, we could make significant improvements.

We must not leave everything to the organizations we have established to make studies, gather information, make contacts, negotiate, and deliberate. We must solicit the help and input of all the people involved. And we must be careful not to be forever telling everyone how things

are and what we think, because then we will never have
time to listen.

Leadership

I conclude this discussion of change, then, by emphasizing something that has not changed at all: the need for
businesspeople to be well informed, so that they can further social interests. Are we able to listen? Are we prepared to look into things? Do we truly wish to act
objectively? Are we interested in the facts? Can we faith-
fully and clearly pass on what we have heard and seen?
And, above all, do we take seriously the people we deal
with? We should all resolve to work harder in these areas.

My final comment is this: decision-making and acting
are becoming more difficult and risky, but they are just
as necessary as they were before. Politics clearly demon-
strates this truth, but the point applies to social and economic areas as well.

Leadership is especially necessary in these times because we cannot depend as much on tradition, position,
and discipline as we have in the past. Those who are
called to be leaders must not take their responsibilities
lightly or try to hide behind real or imagined taboos.
There is no substitute for knowledge, ability, courage,
and wisdom.

APPENDIX

ROYAL DUTCH/SHELL
GROUP OF COMPANIES

STATEMENT
OF
GENERAL
BUSINESS PRINCIPLES

INTRODUCTION

THE NEED HAS BECOME INCREASINGLY CLEAR FOR A statement of the general business principles which underlie the overall conduct of companies of the Royal Dutch/Shell Group consistent with the requirements imposed by the countries in which they operate. The principles outlined in the following statement are not new: they are already embodied—directly or indirectly—in the existing management philosophies of many operating companies, or in personnel management guides, environmental and safety codes, etc., or constitute an implicit part of decision-making. Here, for the first time, they are formulated into a general statement.

1. Objectives

The objectives of the Royal Dutch/Shell group of companies are to engage efficiently, responsibly, and profitably over a significant period in the businesses of oil, gas, chemicals, coal, metals, and related businesses, and to

121

play an active role in the search for and development of other sources of energy.

2. Responsibilities

In addition to the duty of protecting the shareholders' investment and providing an acceptable financial return, these companies have three other interdependent responsibilities:

(a) To employees

To ensure that employees have good, safe working conditions, and fair remuneration and retirement benefits; and to promote the development and best use of human talent and potential, encouraging employee involvement in the planning and directing of their work, and recognizing that success depends on the full contribution of all employees, who in turn must be fairly treated.

(b) To customers

To develop and provide good products and services which are acceptable in quality and price. And to remember that our group has no guaranteed future: Shell companies depend on winning and maintaining customers' support and adequate payment for products and services.

(c) To society

To provide products and services in a manner that shows good citizenship, and that pays proper attention to safety and to social and environmental standards and needs.

These four areas of responsibility form an interdependent whole.

3. The Role of Profit

Profitability is a condition of carrying out these responsibilities and of staying in business. It is a criterion both of efficiency and of the value that people put on Shell products and services. It is essential for the proper allocation of resources, and needed to provide the continuing investment required for effective response to consumer demand and preference. Without profits and a strong financial foundation, it would not be possible to give shareholders a return on their money, to continue to provide a reliable service to customers, to offer proper pay and benefits to employees, or to perform any other kind of worthwhile service to society.

4. The Market Economy

Shell companies work in a wide variety of environments, the nature of which they cannot control. In general, however, over the long run the community can be served most efficiently in a market economy in which customers have a range of choice, and ultimately decide, according to preference, from whom they want to buy and what they want to buy.

The right of governments to legislate social and economic matters is indisputable, but under normal circumstances the requirements of the market are best determined by competition with minimum government intervention.

5. Political Activities

(a) Companies

Companies should always endeavor to act commercially, operating within existing national laws in a socially responsible manner, and avoiding involvement in politics. It is, however, their legitimate right and responsibility to speak publicly on matters that affect the interests of employees, customers, and shareholders, and on matters of general interest to which they can specifically and knowledgeably contribute.

Criteria for making investment decisions, which are essentially economic, include fully considering social and environmental aspects, although the appraisal of the probable security of an investment must include assessments of likely political developments. Decisions, and particularly investment decisions, should be based on commercial criteria, not aimed at influencing political causes or the pattern of particular societies. The latter are the concern of individual citizens and governments, not companies.

(b) Political payments
As a general rule, there are strong reasons why companies should not make payments to political organizations, although in some cases such payments may be legal and a generally accepted practice. In these exceptional cases payments are acceptable provided they are of modest amount, are properly accounted for, and are authorized by the board of the company.

(c) Employees
Certain employees wish to engage in community activities, including running for public office. The company should favorably consider their wishes in those cases in which they do not go against local laws or circumstances.

6. Grants and General Community Projects
The most important contribution that companies can make to the social and material progress of the countries in which they operate is doing their business efficiently.

But companies also need to take a constructive interest in social matters not necessarily related to the business. Opportunities for involvement—for example, through educational assistance or financial donations—will vary depending upon the size of the company concerned, the nature of the environment, and the scope for useful private initiatives.

7. Integrity of Accounting and Bribery
For both ethical and legal reasons, Shell companies follow strict principles regarding the legality of payments they make and the integrity of all accounting records. Offering, paying, or taking bribes are unacceptable practices.

8. Information
The importance of the activities of Shell companies and their impact on national economies and individuals are well recognized. Complete, relevant information about these activities is therefore given to legitimately interested parties, both national and international, but subject to any overriding consideration of confidentiality proper to the protection of the business and the interests of third parties, and the need to avoid wasteful distribution of information.

*   *   *   *   *

The reputation of the Royal Dutch/Shell group of companies depends on the existence of clearly understood principles and responsibilities, and on their daily practical observance in widely differing environments. Through these positive endeavors, we can maintain the highest standards of business behavior.